Baguette
Moments

Baguette Moments

Marvin K. Lucas

Baguette Moments

ISBN: 978-0-9844974-6-1

Unless otherwise indicated, all Scripture references are from the Holy Bible, New International Version, copyright 1973, 1978, 1984 by the International Bible Society. Used by permission of Zondervan Bible Publishers.

Also quoted are Scriptures from the *Holy Bible*, New Living Translation, copyright © 1996, 2004. Used by permission of Tyndale House Publishers, Inc.

Cover and book interior design: Toney C. Mulhollan

Illumination Publishers International
www.ipibooks.com
6010 Pinecreek Ridge Court
Spring, Texas 77379-2513, USA

TABLE OF CONTENTS

TABLE OF CONTENTS

Acknowledgements

I want to thank my wife Sharisse, for her love and patience, and for her support in helping me fulfill this dream. Her excerpt in this book reflects how pivotal she is in my life and ministry.

Jeremy Lindley, Jason Lugo and Carlos Castillo are great friends, and I am indebted to them for putting their trust in me.

Thanks to the editorial staff at Illumination Publishers which include DeAnne Leonard, Jerri Newman, Toney Mulhollan and Gordon Ferguson for their helpful input on the manuscript.

A special thanks to Gordon Ferguson for his expertise and friendship through the years. This is a true testimony to God.

These people's real-life contributions to this book are invaluable. I am appreciative to all the people I have served and led over the years, especially the DFW Church. I am truly grateful for their refinement and love.

I am especially grateful for the East London Church accommodating us whilst preparing to plant a church in Norwich, England.

Foreword

Marvin's book, *Baguette Moments*, is unique—just like its author! I've known Marvin for a number of years, having worked together in a church in Boston, and then staying in touch with each other in the years since we both left there. Interestingly, in Dallas, where Marvin has ministered for the past eight years, he has been friends with my brother-in-law and his family, who are in the same church with Marvin. So, God has kept us tied together in spite of the distance between us geographically.

Being asked to write Forewords for books is always a special privilege. As an author myself, I know that you invite people to write introductions to your books who mean a lot to you personally. Knowing that makes this invitation an honor for me, especially since Marvin has been a very special friend to me for many years now, and it is his first book.

As I said, Marvin and his book are truly unique. The book is unique in several ways. One, it uses a term that we don't often hear, entrustment, although it is a great word and various forms of it are found repeatedly in the Bible. Some form of "entrust" is found 39 times in the NIV Bible. The basic meaning of entrustment is to "confer a trust on" or "to commit to another with confidence." The concept of entrusting another with what is precious to you (God's Word and work in this case) paints a beautiful word picture. As Marvin develops his main premise, the idea of entrustment is really about pouring your life into the lives of others on an individual basis as you help train them to become more and more like Jesus. More specifically, it is all about leaders raising up other leaders in a church context, but it also applies similar principles to marriage and family relationships.

Two, the book is unique in how Marvin describes situations in and out of the Bible. In reading stories in the Bible, you normally have to use your imagination to fill in the likely contexts of those stories. The way Marvin does this takes you down some new and unexpected avenues. He makes you see various passages in backgrounds that you have not thought of before. Since all such supplying of contexts comes from one's imagination, they cannot be proved—but neither can they be disproved. Thus, it makes for a tantalizing and provocative read. I can promise you that you will not be bored!

Three, the uniqueness comes through a balanced blend of providing both specific critiques and specific recommendations. Marvin is writing from a broad perspective of religious training and experiences. You will find yourself reading the critiques and asking the question, "Is he talking about me?" (or "about my church?"). The fact that he leaves you wondering at times helps you wrestle with the proper applications. You actually have to think and to evaluate yourself, your ministry, your marriage and your family. That is always quite a worthwhile endeavor. On the other hand, the many practical recommendations are explained primarily by his personal examples or the examples of others with whom he has worked. It is far more practical than theoretical for this reason.

The style of the book helps explains Marvin's uniqueness as a person. He leads you down unpredictable paths as you read, which helps maintain your interest. Perhaps he is most unique in the nature of his example of living what he writes about. His example of not only trusting people, but entrusting them with all that is dear to him stands out clearly. The man practices what he preaches on this subject. Entrustment is a word that is pregnant with meaning, and you won't have to read long to see that. It is an art form, not simply a spiritual exercise, and one that is crying out to be practiced far more than is currently the case. Simply put, it is the Master's plan of changing lives and affecting eternity through fallible human beings. Marvin is dedicated heart and soul to this plan, and if reading his book doesn't persuade you, the fault will be yours. He makes his case biblically, practically and personally. Hopefully you will "get it" without having to have too many baguette moments! (Since you don't yet know what that means, turn to Marvin's Introduction and start reading!)

—Gordon Ferguson
Phoenix, Arizona

Introduction

I came to America with ten dollars in my pocket! How can a twenty-two-year-old "man" confidently come to a foreign country with so little and believe that he can live the American dream? Well, over the last twenty years, God has allowed me to far exceed what I could have hoped for in the American dream, but this only came about by way of God's strong hand of empowerment and protection throughout my life.

My "Tale of Entrustment" started when I was five, when I walked to school by myself in inner city London, and He protected me every step of the way. When I was eleven, I started working my first job at a local corner grocery store. And as if working at eleven were not enough responsibility, I was often left alone to run the entire store by myself. It was not clear to me then that God was working his empowerment process through such circumstances. At thirteen, I was working in a restaurant as a dessert boy. By the age of sixteen, I was "working the middle" at this same restaurant. This position entailed calling out the orders to professional chefs and telling them when and how things needed to be cooked. Each of the chefs was old enough to be my father, but I was respected by these men because I was good at what I did. I was only sixteen years old! By this time, I was able to buy my own clothes and support myself.

As I got older, God continued to protect and empower me as I traveled throughout Europe—even through my poor decision making. By the time I was twenty, I decided to work in a bed-and-breakfast in Belgium, where I was exploited—working 80 hours per week for only $100! So I eventually teamed up with my friend, Bob, and we travelled together throughout Europe living on credit. We visited France, the Netherlands, Luxemburg, Switzerland, Italy and Germany, and eventually ended up broke, scraping out a meager living. Many a time we ran out of a restaurant or hotel without paying!

One time, we sold our watches just to put gas in the car. On another occasion, after a storm, I opted to shovel sand on the Cote d'Azur in the south of France, simply to make money to live. I did not want to call home for help because of my pride.

Although it began very strongly, my relationship with Bob deteriorated until I was no longer welcome in his apartment while living in Brussels. Being a foreign man, in a foreign country, trying to understand a foreign language and with nowhere to stay, I was virtually living on the streets. Realizing that my predicament was the result of my poor choices, I went out and began to beg for money.

But God was not finished with me yet. I started asking for change to use the phone. I was able to get enough money for a can of Coke and a baguette (pronounced bag-get), which is a small loaf of French bread. This was the lowest, and one of the more defining points of my life. At the end of this chain of events, I was alone, homeless, broke and clearly humbled. When times are hard today, I reflect on my "baguette" moment.

During this time, I met a friend who was a professional drummer, who surprisingly understood my plight, gave up his bed for me and slept on the floor! He also gave me $200 to get back to England. So coming to America one year later with only $10 was not really a daunting challenge to me.

So why do I share my tale? I believe that I was able to adapt and adjust to my surroundings because I had been empowered and entrusted at an early age. If you are a parent, you may be freaking out because you think I am suggesting that you send your child walking through the urban sprawl at age five—but don't miss the point! Many of us feel that, with a kind of magical switch, we can become a superhero or super-Christian overnight. Many believe that they will have some sort of out-of-the-blue epiphany and be transformed into someone mature and fearless like David, or sacrificial like Abraham. But it just doesn't work that way! David's story teaches that sometimes we need to slay the lion and the bear before we can take on the Goliath. Abraham had to sacrifice his home and his land in Ur before he could get to the point of being willing to sacrifice his son Isaac.

This book focuses on the entrustment processes of God.

When I examine my life, it becomes obvious that God has worked through friends, strangers and even my own stupidity, to bring about my life change. As I reflect on these processes, I see God's protection from the streets of Brussels with a baguette and a can of Coke, to the many ways he has empowered me to arrive at where I stand today—a faithful man of God. I hope my words will inspire you to tap into the predestined life of entrustment which God has in store for you. Are you ready to turn on the floodgates of faith?

Part One

What is Entrustment?

Chapter

1

What is Faith?

faith is unutterable trust in God,
trust which never dreams that He will not stand by us.[1]

☞ The Definition

Allegiance to duty or a person: loyalty
Fidelity to one's promise
Sincerity of intentions
Firm belief in something for which there is no proof
Complete trust

Complete trust? Really! Whoever trusts completely? This type of trust exists only in Disney movies, fairy tales or utopian societies found on other planets. Planet Earth is filled with realities that promote mistrust: injustices, racial biases as well as emotional, physical and spiritual abuses—often by those in authority such as parents, family members, employers, ministers, mentors and friends.

Complete trust is one of those things that sounds so good, but no one really expects to see it lived out. However true this may be for the present age, it must be noted that, in order to have the faith God has intended for each one of us, we must get to the point where we can completely trust him. If your life is similar to my own, this can seem like an impossible task.

My upbringing and life have been riddled with dysfunction and instability, but in order to understand me, it is important to understand where my parents came from. My father grew up on the east side of Cleveland, Ohio, in a predominately African American community and in a religious household. His mother, my grandmother, played the piano and led the choir at a couple of the local churches. This meant she was involved in one or two church services on any given Sunday, and my dad usually had to tag along. So my dad had quite a religious upbringing.

My dad eventually graduated from high school and was headed to college, but he decided to enlist in the U.S. Air Force instead. It is likely that my dad felt stifled, and as a young man looking for his own identity, he made this decision. When he had only two weeks left at home, he told his parents of his decision, and this caused a major rift in the family.

While based in England, my dad met and married an English woman, my mother. Interracial unions, however, were not popular in the early 1960s. Growing up, we had no religion or church influence in our home; and as a child, I had no exposure to spiritual learning. I cannot remember even seeing a Bible in our home. In light of my dad's religious upbringing, this may seem shocking, but his actions showed a major backlash and rebellion against being forced into religion as a child. My parents, being so young, fell into many of the typical traps of young parenthood.

The 60s and 70s were wild times for us as a family, and only perpetuated domestic instability and uncertainty. The reaction to this disarray was that often as siblings we would fight and even come to physical blows on many occasions. It was extremely hard for me to find a refuge and to trust anyone. I would spend hours outside on the streets or in my room by myself, with little or no interaction with my parents or siblings. This tendency for isolation has been a challenge to overcome even to this day.

Growing up relatively poor, I started to fend for myself. By the age of eleven, I was working and paying for my own clothes, not needing any allowance. Over time, this domestic instability led me to be a child full of anger. I often fought at school. I remember one fight that started when a kid made some racial statements about me, and it ended when he went to the hospital. I put his head through the wall! As I grew older, my pagan lifestyle grew to full-blown immorality, drunkenness and other types of wild living. I constantly mocked Christianity and even persecuted those who shared their faith or even talked about God. I was a loner, full of hate. My worldview had begun to take shape: "No one can be completely trusted. No one!"

When I was twenty-two years old, a wind of change began to stir. I jumped on a plane and came to America, arriving in Cleveland, Ohio. One year later, I moved to Los Angeles, where I met a young lady named Sharisse. Shortly after we met, we began dating.

One day at a modeling shoot, Sharisse was reached out to by another model who happened to be a Christian. They started a friendship and Sharisse began to go to church and study the Bible. I thought it was cute that she was doing the "church thing," until it began affecting my life! Sharisse would study the Scriptures with the women from the church, and then come back and try to change me. She asked me to stop swearing, but having no fear of God, I cursed even more! But one day, after a Bible study, Sharisse's new conviction not to have sex outside of marriage was "the straw that broke the camel's back" for me. When she told me, "We can't have sex anymore," that was the deal breaker!

This "church thing" had gone too far. Consequently, we broke up, which obviously broke Sharisse's heart and mine as well. At this point, I did not trust my parents, women or other men. I had no friends—and certainly no God. My worldview was confirmed: "No one can be completely trusted." I barely even trusted myself, especially when I was drinking. I had reached a crossroads. After a few days passed, I realized that I really missed Sharisse, even though I had other female relationships. So I called her, and she pleaded with me to visit her church.

Visiting Sharisse's church was not a good experience initially. My first inclination was actually to try and take her out of the church! To no one's surprise, I was extremely cynical and critical of everything and everyone there. One of the ministers eventually invited us over for dinner and asked me if I had any questions. I said, "Yes! Why can't we have sex?" This is a hard question to answer for someone who does not believe the truths found in the Bible.

In the ensuing weeks, God started to soften my heart and open my eyes. I began to notice the sincere friendships and devoted marriages in the church. For me, this made the Bible real, and this realization encouraged me to study the Scriptures. My Bible studies began on a Monday, and by the following Sunday, April 28, 1991, I was baptized near Santa Monica Pier. God moved quickly and powerfully in my heart, and six months later, I was married to Sharisse. At the time of this writing, we have been happily married for 18 years and have two kids. In this life, I have been abused, and I have abused others. Many people, under similar circumstances, could be full of bitterness and rage because of that. It is only by God's grace and his redemptive process that I am not. I had to trust him, trust Sharisse and trust others before I could grow to have the faith I have today. One real sign of this transformation in my life is my relationship with my dad. Today, I actually give him hugs and tell him that I love him. You have no idea what a miracle this is!

Brothers, sisters and friends, the reality is that complete trust is the essence of faith, and without it, we are only empty religious shells, simply going through the motions and building shallow relationships, which are never enough. In hopes of bringing us one step closer to where God intends us to be, I would like to examine three principles: mistrust, trust and entrust.

Mistrust

Peace will elude us if, on our journey to find it, we carry baggage of suspicion and mistrust or fear. [2]

Mistrust has become a staple of our society. Many of the political leaders of America have been given the lowest approval ratings in decades. We all seem to be caught up in the battle. Our school systems and healthcare systems are fighting for funds, educators are pitted against families, and families of "normal" children are pitted against families of children with disabilities—all competing for scarce resources. We have seen scandals in churches that are widely publicized by the media. Hurts experienced in the church cut deeply because we believe it to be a safe place (and I do believe it is a *safer* place than the world). Postmodern idealism states that truth is what you believe, and only you can know what is true for you. We see this in corporate slogans like, "Have it *your* way", "*You* deserve a break today", and "*I'm* lovin' it." We have created a "me" generation with our "I" phones and "I" pods. This mindset kills the sense of community and "one-anotherness" which are mainstays at the foundation of Christian beliefs. Mistrust has slowly and steadily brought us to a self-centered and overly suspicious society.

Signs of mistrust include: insecurity around others, critical-ness (especially toward authority), conditional relationships, a lack of openness (even in long-term relationships), a controlling nature and a deep sense of aloneness. Mistrust kills community and it kills faith.

Trust

TRUST IS A LEARNED BEHAVIOR. Susie is one of the most trustworthy people I know; I trust her with my life. Imagine she is in a long line at the bank. The individual behind her is holding $1,000 cash with a completed deposit ticket. This person is obviously anxious and in a hurry, so Susie politely offers to help, saying, "If you are just depositing your money, I could take care of it for you." What do you think the odds are for a complete stranger to hand over $1,000 and then go on with their day without giving a second thought to their money? Yet, is Susie any less trustworthy if the individual refuses to give her their money to deposit? No, the person just has not learned to trust Susie. Trust doesn't come naturally to any of us; trust has to be learned. In the same way we learn to trust our parents or other people in our lives, we must also learn to trust God.[3]

We all must trust! When I drive down the street, I trust that the car on the other side of the road will keep to the other side of those two yellow lines in the center of the road. When I go through an intersection, I trust that the 18-wheeler will stop at the red light as I drive forward on green. There are many things we do in life, assuming that the other party is going to obey the laws and local ordinances. We all trust, because if we didn't, we would not be able to leave our homes. I would bet that if the media showed every car crash every day, we would never put another key in the ignition. And I do believe if we watched television much less, we would be a much more trusting society. We decide who to trust (which is an act of faith), because we learn who is trustworthy by their words and their actions. A person who trusts has certain positive attributes—they are secure, decisive, obedient, verbally supportive, relational and faithful.

When you trust someone, it is based on mutual terms that both parties must keep; it is non-binding, relationally oriented and takes a combined effort on both parts. With trust, one can pull it back at any time when one's boundaries have been violated.

Entrustment
☞ The Definition

> To deliver something in trust
>
> To bestow a trust on
>
> To commit to another with confidence

Entrustment is different than trusting. To entrust means to give up total control to another party. There are no mutual terms. This is a one-way transaction with no conditions—to entrust oneself to another through total surrender to their will. In conclusion, mistrust and trust are based on conditions, real or imagined. To entrust, on the other hand, is all about empowering others by relinquishing total control/power to them. I remember a time when I entrusted myself to a couple, then later discovered how much deeper their level of trust was in me than mine was in them. Let me share that story with you.

A Personal Story of Trust: Yura and Yulia

I recently returned from a conference in Kiev, Ukraine (in the former Soviet Union) and to be honest, I had not been looking forward to the trip. Like most Eastern European or Eurasian countries, this one was not especially picturesque, nor the people very friendly! But this was an opportunity that I might never have again, so I knew I should go. I was initially surprised to see almost no people of color there in my five days visiting. I only saw two people of color (one African and another lady who was interracial). I think our conference attendees from America may have tripled the minority population in Kiev! After visiting many countries throughout Europe, I can say that Ukraine has the lowest percentage of people who can speak English. They are not especially friendly folk who will say "Hi," smile or nod their head as a cordial greeting. In Kiev, people generally do not even look at you; there is no eye contact, not even a little nod to show that you exist! This city, in general, can be a cold place and quite unwelcoming to outsiders.

However, in the church I visited, I saw a refreshing contrast! The Christians were hospitable and generous, even with the little they had. I was given a mug, a key chain and refrigerator magnets by total strangers. The sincere gratitude for our fellowship was overwhelming, and I was convicted by their generosity after my initial reluctance to go to this country.

The day before we left for home, we went to church with the locals and those at the conference. Afterward, I decided to tag along with a couple I knew from Boston and have lunch with them and some of the native Ukrainians. Among those who joined us was a couple named Yura and Yulia, whom I had not met before. Fortunately, the wife spoke excellent English and translated for the whole group. During lunch, I wanted to find out a little more about this couple. I eventually learn that they lived about 70 km (45 miles) outside Kiev and worshipped in a house church setting with a handful of other Christians. They shared that they had been married for five years and had a three-year-old daughter.

As the lunch was coming to an end, out of the blue I said, "I want to go to your home today!" Although I barely knew this couple, the Holy Spirit was prompting me to invite myself over. They initially thought I was joking, but I repeated myself three times, and they were elated to have me come to their town. I asked, "So where did you park your car?" And to my surprise, they responded, "We have no car!" So I had to embark on a subway train and two bus rides to their home, which took nearly two hours. The whole time I was thinking to myself, "What did I just ask for? I am 6' 2", 255 pounds, and these buses were small and packed." I had to sit facing the aisle because I could not sit straight due to the lack of legroom. It was not until the second bus ride that it dawned on me that I was by myself with a couple I did not know; I had no idea where I was going or how to get back; I was in a country where no one spoke English; and being a person of color, it was not like I could just blend in with the natives! The Lord helped me to surrender my will! But actually, I felt safe—remembering that God had protected me when I was 21, in Belgium, with the *baguette and a can of Coke*—plus, I was actually enjoying this fellowship.

We arrived at the town where they lived, *White Church*. This town had been besieged by enemy forces many years before, and the only structure left standing was one white church, hence the name. They took me to a park and we prayed. While there, we met another couple who had been part of their house church but had left the Lord a couple of years previously. Thankfully, they had recently expressed the desire to come back. We went to their apartment and studied Scriptures on marriage, parenting and repentance. I was blown away by their humility. There was no defensiveness or rebuttals at all. They simply responded with one word—"Amen" (so be it). Their meekness was very challenging to me as I reflected on my own pride with others, especially with my wife. Being around these folk almost made me question my own salvation, for I knew that God hates pride. He made that clear in Proverbs 8:13, which states: "To fear the LORD is to hate evil; I hate pride and arrogance, evil behavior and perverse speech."

Yura and Yulia showed me what it was like to be "poor in spirit".[4] This couple had no television, no computers, no iPods or iPads, no cell phones or even hot water, but the little they had, they freely shared with me. They were rich in gratitude, hospitality and trust. They trusted because they had nothing to lose, no image or possessions to protect, and no pretense. I believe that this couple trusted me as a stranger because they were not brainwashed and bombarded by the media with their stories of the horrors of society and their constant reminder of how poor and unhappy people are without a certain product. I believe that the West has become so mistrusting (partly because of the paranoia engendered by the media) that we constantly feel like our next door neighbor may be a pedophile or a rapist. We feel that if we have a stranger in our home, they are probably going to steal something; or maybe we think our house is not ready for hospitality because the curtains are not new enough or the carpet is not clean enough! Brothers and sisters, this is the deceitfulness of wealth[5] that chokes out community and hinders the trusting of one another. I hope you can learn something from Yulia and Yura as I did.

Due to the economic crisis, many of the foreign investors have pulled out of Kiev, their currency has lost significant value and, consequently, many have lost their jobs. Yulia and Yura were considering taking their chances and moving to the West for a "better life," but this was my response in a message I sent them via Yulia's workplace email:

> Yura and Yulia; many people want to come to America and live a better life, but many fall into the trap of greed, comfort and debauchery. Many in the church here have become lukewarm and have succumbed to the world and lost their joy.[6] The "merry faces" that you see in the Kiev church is a blessing that far outweighs the comforts and pleasures of a "better life." You might be poor,[7] but you are rich. We Americans are rich, but we are poor. I left the Ukraine considering my life and was envious of what you guys have in the church there.
>
> I want to encourage you to remember that our treasure is in Heaven.[8]
>
> "Therefore, my brothers/sisters, you whom I love and long for, my joy and crown, that is how you should stand firm in the Lord, dear friends" (Philippians 4:1)!
>
> Paul writes this to show where his joy could be found, and

it was in the brothers and sisters, not in things, jobs or the Hryvna (local currency). Our joy is in the disciples and in heaven. When we take our eyes off the prize, we will lose faith and waver. Keep your eyes on the prize!

"Since, then, you have been raised with Christ, set your hearts on things above, where Christ is seated at the right hand of God. Set your minds on things above, not on earthly things" (Colossians 3:1-2).

Keep the faith and the (merry) face!

—MKL

Friends, it's time to start trusting. As you could probably see in this story, entrustment gave birth to trust. If we want others to trust us, we have to start by exercising some entrustment in others.

Since writing this, I have learned that Yulia and Yura have lost their jobs and their apartment due to the recession, which has been significantly worse there than here. Adding to their hardship, the Russian government has turned off the gas supply to the Ukraine during the peak of winter. Please, pray for them.

Chapter

2

Free Will—Crisps and CDs

I love choices. When I go to my local supermarket, I enjoy the freedom of choosing my favorite crisps (chips): cheese and onion, salt and vinegar, plain, barbeque or one of many other flavors. Just imagine if one day I show up and the store manager said, "The only flavor you can have is barbeque." Yes, barbeque is okay, but my favorite is salt and vinegar. However, he insists that barbeque is his favorite and everyone must eat them. There are a couple of responses I could have. I can be a "people pleaser" and take the barbeque and tolerate it, although I know that over time, I would develop a low-grade resentment towards the manager. I would feel forced to accept his selection, and I might come to dislike barbeque chips altogether. Or in my pride, I could be stubborn and insist on my salt and vinegar crisps, argue for several minutes and end up leaving the store with no crisps at all, vowing never to return. All this is to say that we love our choices and not having them makes us feel that our God-given free will has been violated.

Yes, God gave us free will. God gave Adam and Eve choices. Entrustment involves respecting an individual's free will and power to make decisions on his own. Consider the great Paradise and the freedom Adam and Eve were given to roam the whole Garden, which probably spanned miles. God's entrustment literally allowed them to do virtually anything they wanted, with one exception: a fruit tree. They could touch the tree but not its fruit. Satan cunningly persuaded Adam and Eve that the limitation regarding this one tree was somehow more important than the complete freedom granted in the rest of the Garden.

When my daughter was a toddler, she would test her boundaries as to what was safe and acceptable behavior and what was not. Putting Barbie accessories in the electrical outlets was a no-no! We made our home "child safe" and put away anything that would break or harm our precious child. But I deliberately kept my two stand-alone stacks of CDs next to the television. She could play anywhere else in the house, but where did she choose to go? You guessed it. Those twin towers of temptation taunted this terrible two-year-old, and many a time she took them and *shared* them with the living room floor, but I still did not move them. A battle of the wills began! After a while, she learned how to please mummy and daddy by obeying and by not touching the CDs. This exercise was not a matter of physical life or death, but it served to establish the principle that you cannot always have or touch what you see! If parents do not teach their kids these principles, they become nervous slaves to their children's whims, putting one thing after another out of reach, or worse, expecting others to do so because their children have not learned boundaries concerning what not to touch.

The other day, a visiting two-year-old displayed no regard for our furniture. He jumped on our cushions, climbed all over the back of the couch, and stood on our coffee table, not even looking back at the parents to see if this was acceptable. When I corrected the child, he looked at me as though I had spoiled his ultimate *Chuck E. Cheese* adventure! The parents corrected their son and expected him to magically begin to obey their commands just because he was at my home. How far this was from the truth! The child threw a tantrum, and you can imagine how ugly the situation became. If he didn't obey his parents in his own home, how could he be realistically expected to obey them in someone else's home?

You cannot always touch nor have what you see. How many people are in debt because they don't respect this principle; how many have committed adultery because they lack this principle; or how many have breached a trust because they have no regard for the boundaries of others. God was teaching Adam and Eve a lesson as the world was being populated: "You are going to see things that you want but cannot have." The three sins Paul saw as community sins that must be expelled from the fellowship are impurity, immorality and greed.[9] I believe this describes how careful we should be in exercising our freedom in Christ. We do have many freedoms, but all God-given boundaries are for our own good.

Everything is permissible for me"—but not everything is beneficial. "Everything is permissible for me"—but I will not be mastered by anything (1 Corinthians 6:12).

My Way or Yahweh!

In the Bible, we see many passages about the will of God. Many preachers preach every Sunday on how to obey the will of God, or "Yahweh" (pronounced Yah-Way). The opposite of Yahweh is "My Way." In the previous chapter, I touched on the idea that our society is "me-centered." Free will often puts fear in a preacher's heart, and in a parent's heart. In the case of the preacher, if he wants the church to flourish, a sense of community must be built. However, selfish people can become toxic and contaminate what one has built. In the case of the parent, if they see their child establishing their own will outside of God's will, the parent tends to panic and in "love," become controlling. During this time, the child has to find out who they are and what they believe; and if a parent is of a controlling nature, this can be a heated time as the battle of the wills ensues.

Remember, a child has to become a sinner before becoming a saint. Many youth ministries and parents fight this process and rush their kids into the church. This often compounds the problem. The result will be that the son or daughter becomes a Christian, but later acts like a pagan due to the parents *willing* their kids into the church before their child's own will has been allowed to develop. This process inevitably causes "spiritual birth defects." Once the child is a Christian and begins acting rebelliously, it is obvious that it would have been better to tolerate pagan behavior longer in a son or daughter rather than pushing them into the church before they were ready to make this decision of their own free will. In the meantime, the child still has yet to *find* themselves.

God has entrusted us with free will so that we can learn from our experiences and choices, and ultimately choose him. It is sad to see in God's church that some people merely cohere in fulfilling a corporate will or a preacher's vision for their life. I am not saying that we should not have a corporate will and expectation; these belong to community righteousness and conduct. However, the individual's will must always be honored; as leaders, we ministers must persuade and reason and inspire others to do God's will.[10] Guilt, manipulation and controlling techniques will always ultimately lead to revolt, and will stifle joy and personal creativity in Christ. This is why my dad has not stepped in a church for 45 years; he did not like the controlling nature of his upbringing. In contrast, I had never read the Bible or was forced to go to church. I lived a life of sin and free will, and when approached by the truth, I personally had no deep-rooted resentment toward Christianity. Therefore, once I heard the truth, I surrendered my life to Christ and was baptized in a week. Two stories: one child grew up with oppressive religion, and one without! Who is better off now? I was free to make choices and learned through my own free will that God's will was the only way.

God has clearly displayed his entrustment by never forcing His will on us. Even Jesus had to fight between choosing his will and God's will in the Garden of Gethsemane. God wants us to turn to him because of his mercy and grace. Paul writes that when we surrender to God's love, great things begin to happen:

> *Therefore, I urge you, brothers, in view of God's mercy, to offer your bodies as living sacrifices, holy and pleasing to God— this is your spiritual act of worship. Do not conform any longer to the pattern of this world, but be transformed by the renewing of your mind. Then you will be able to test and approve what God's will is—his good, pleasing and perfect will* (Romans 12:1-2).

We must offer ourselves; we should not be guilt ridden, forced, or manipulated. God inspires us to come to him by the realization of his grace in our life (verse 1). God wants us to turn to him having no strings, terms or conditions attached.[11] God's love will bring us back with his powerful grace. Another favorite passage of mine on this subject is Romans 2:4, which reads: "Or do you show contempt for the riches of his kindness, tolerance and patience, not realizing that God's kindness leads you toward repentance?"

There are times when one must rebuke, warn and admonish, but we cannot afford to forget that God's loving whisper of kindness can break the most stubborn heart.

Chapter

3

We Have Been Entrusted

The Parable of the Talents

"*Again, it will be like a man going on a journey, who called his servants and entrusted his property to them. To one he gave five talents of money, to another two talents, and to another one talent, each according to his ability. Then he went on his journey. The man who had received the five talents went at once and put his money to work and gained five more. So also, the one with the two talents gained two more. But the man who had received the one talent went off, dug a hole in the ground and hid his master's money.*

"*After a long time the master of those servants returned and settled accounts with them. The man who had received the five talents brought the other five. 'Master,' he said, 'you entrusted me with five talents. See, I have gained five more.'*

"*His master replied, 'Well done, good and faithful servant! You have been faithful with a few things; I will put you in charge of many things. Come and share your master's happiness!'*

"*The man with the two talents also came. 'Master,' he said, 'you entrusted me with two talents; see, I have gained two more.' "His master replied, 'Well done, good and faithful servant! You have been faithful with a few things; I will put you in charge of many things. Come and share your master's happiness!'*

"*Then the man who had received the one talent came.*

'Master,' he said, 'I knew that you are a hard man, harvesting where you have not sown and gathering where you have not scattered seed. So I was afraid and went out and hid your talent in the ground. See, here is what belongs to you.'

"His master replied, 'You wicked, lazy servant! So you knew that I harvest where I have not sown and gather where I have not scattered seed? Well then, you should have put my money on deposit with the bankers, so that when I returned I would have received it back with interest.

"'Take the talent from him and give it to the one who has the ten talents. For everyone who has will be given more and he will have an abundance. Whoever does not have, even what he has will be taken from him. And throw that worthless servant outside, into the darkness, where there will be weeping and gnashing of teeth' (Matthew 25:14-30).

In Matthew 25, Jesus uses two parables to describe the Kingdom of God. We see in this parable that the owner has left and *entrusted* the talents to his servants. He expects a return from his gift. When we read this passage, the ones with five and two talents verbally stated that they were entrusted with a gift and put it to work. The one with one talent did nothing and hid it, and he was severely punished for it. Jesus has left us in charge of his Kingdom and we have been entrusted to multiply it. As mentioned earlier, there is an innate danger in entrustment. One surrenders his power, possessions and/or principles into the care of another. This individual is free to do whatever they want with what has been given them. Isn't it incredible that the master entrusted these men with money? Isn't it more amazing that Jesus has entrusted us with so much more than money?

Another passage of entrustment can be found in the letter to the Ephesians:

Praise be to the God and Father of our Lord Jesus Christ, who has blessed us in the heavenly realms with every spiritual blessing in Christ. For he chose us in him before the creation of the world to be holy and blameless in his sight. In love he predestined *us to be adopted as his sons through Jesus Christ, in accordance with his pleasure and will—to the praise of his glorious grace, which he has freely given us in the One he loves. In him we have redemption through his blood, the forgiveness of sins, in accordance with the riches of God's grace that he lavished on us with all wisdom and understanding. And he made known to us the mystery of his will according to his good pleasure, which he purposed in Christ, to be put into effect when the times will have reached their fulfillment—to bring all things in heaven and on earth together under one head, even Christ.*

In him we were also chosen, having been predestined according to the plan of him who works out everything in conformity with the purpose of his will, in order that we, who were the first to hope in Christ, might be for the praise of his glory. And you also were included in Christ when you heard the word of truth, the gospel of your salvation. Having believed, you were marked in him with a seal, the promised Holy Spirit, who is a deposit guaranteeing our inheritance until the redemption of those who are God's possession—to the praise of his glory (Ephesians 1:3-14).

Before the beginning of time, God has entrusted us with his eternal blessing, his glorious grace, his wisdom, his understanding, his mystery, his inheritance, his salvation and even his very own Spirit. But what if we mess it all up, completely reject it or use it for evil? The beauty of entrustment is that we *can* do all those things, but the Father still *trusts* us with them.

First of all, like the Jews, we have been entrusted with the very words of God.[12] Being in America, we have the freedom of speech and religion. It is an honor to be entrusted with God's wisdom and guidance, but history tells us that men have often used God's Word more like a butter knife than a surgeon's scalpel. Shouldn't God be a little more careful to whom he entrusts his Word? On the contrary, he continues to offer it freely, continuously hoping and trusting that the entrusted individual will handle it properly. "So then, men ought to regard us as servants of Christ and as those *entrusted* with the secret things of God."[13]

We are entrusted with the secrets of God. Isn't he just a little worried that we might "spill the beans?" Again, that's the nature of entrustment. Doesn't it feel good to be believed in and trusted, knowing that you have a special possession and task? Matthew 13:11 also tells us that we have also been given "the knowledge of the secrets of the kingdom of heaven." What are these secrets? Do we know these secrets? Do we keep these secrets to ourselves? Do we feel that we know more than others? The Bible states we have been given something extra as Christians! "This will take place on the day when God will judge men's secrets through Jesus Christ, as my gospel declares."[14] This Scripture does not talk about us being given secrets, but Christ exposing men's secrets on that day, the secrets of the Kingdom of Heaven. Obviously, entrustment carries obligation and opportunity with it!

Our Faith Is Enough!

Dear friends, although I was very eager to write to you about the salvation we share, I felt I had to write and urge you to contend for the faith that was once for all entrusted to the saints (Jude 1:3).

We have been entrusted with faith. Yet, we can take faith for granted. Faith is an essential spiritual commodity for salvation. Jesus tells his loyal followers, "Well done, good and faithful servant!" Faithful—full of faith! You can see that a person is full of faith when their faith bubbles over into the lives of others. God has entrusted you with the best that he has to offer. "Now it is required that those who have been given a trust must prove faithful."[15] Have you been faithful with what God has entrusted into your care? Have you taken the risk of entrusting others?

Part Two

Jesus
and the
Apostles

Chapter

4

Jesus the Entruster

*One of those days Jesus went out to a mountainside to pray, and **spent the night praying to God**. When morning came, he called his disciples to him and chose twelve of them, whom he also designated apostles: Simon (whom he named Peter), his brother Andrew, James, John, Philip, Bartholomew, Matthew, Thomas, James son of Alphaeus, Simon who was called the Zealot, Judas son of James, and Judas Iscariot, who became a traitor* (Luke 6:12-16).

Is this the best that Jesus could do after a full night of prayer? Did God not hear his prayer, or was he asleep? Think about the background of some of the twelve apostles: John, Peter and Andrew were fishermen (uneducated); Matthew was a tax collector (basically, a robber); Simon was a Zealot (assassin); and Judas stole from Jesus and eventually betrayed him. Later, Jesus called Saul the Pharisee to be an apostle (earlier, a murderer of Christians). Is this the best that the Son of God could do? After all, the Bible tells us that he could call down six legions of angels at a snap of his fingers! And after the Passion, all authority on heaven and earth was given to him. And do you mean to tell me that this is all he could come up with to be his closest followers! Moreover, I think it is an understatement to call these men "unschooled and ordinary men." So exactly why did Jesus choose these men?

For three years, Jesus worked tirelessly with the Twelve, and from them received a lot of broken promises. Even at their last meal together, they all said that they would not leave him. Major setbacks with Peter included his understanding of Jesus' divinity, and yet in the next breath, rebuking Jesus for saying he would die and rise again.[16] The twelve had nearly a constant lack of faith. On a few occasions, Jesus even found more faith in a prostitute, a Samaritan and a centurion than he did in any of these men! Jesus, are you sure that *these* are the men you want to entrust and empower? Have you forgotten their past or even *their* recent track record of faithlessness? No, these are not the kind of people you would consider to be ideal candidates for leading your small group, let alone ushering in the Kingdom of God.

One thing I love about the Bible is that it is real. Even Jesus would get "fed up" sometimes, as we see in this passage:

> *They discussed this with one another and said, "It is because we have no bread." Aware of their discussion, Jesus asked them: "Why are you talking about having no bread? Do you still not see or understand? Are your hearts hardened?* (Mark 8:16-18).

Jesus had fed 9,000 people with a handful of loaves and a few fish. Yet, only hours later, they were complaining about having no food! John states that if he wrote out all the miracles that Jesus performed, there would not be enough room to house all of the books it would take. So when we consider just the ones we can read about—including his transformation, walking on water and raising people from the dead —and the twelve were still lacking faith after witnessing them, we might just understand the dissatisfaction that Jesus felt in them. Then the disciples tried to heal a young boy and could not due to their lack of faith, after which Jesus responded: "O unbelieving generation," Jesus replied, "How long shall I stay with you? How long shall I put up with you? Bring the boy to me."[17]

Jesus continued to show his frustration with his disciples. Jesus had entrusted some of the worst followers a leader could ever have, at least from man's perspective. These twelve men fell away from the faith and walked away from Jesus:

> *Then Jesus told them, "This very night you will all fall away on account of me, for it is written: "I will strike the shepherd, and the sheep of the flock will be scattered.' But after I have risen, I will go ahead of you into Galilee." Peter replied, "Even if all fall away on account of you, I never will." "I tell you the truth,"* Jesus answered, "this very night, before the rooster crows, you will disown me three times." But Peter declared, "Even if I have to die with you, I will never disown you." And all the other disciples said the same* (Matthew 26:31-32).

If Jesus was the CEO of an earthly corporation and produced this return on his investment after three years, he would have been fired. If he was a professor and all of his students were failing after three years, people would think he should never teach again, for obviously it would not seem to be his gift! I have been in the ministry for close to two decades, and I could not tolerate this type of fruitless behavior from a leader for more than a couple of months. For Jesus, three years passed and he was facing the cross, yet not one of the twelve was showing any sign of promise. To make matters worse, Judas showed his true colors of betrayal.

It may have been more for himself than for his disciples that Jesus stayed and prayed on the mountainside the whole night! Praying for his own patience and to have a longsuffering spirit with this ragtag bunch! I suspect that Jesus probably had other followers who appeared to be more highly qualified for the position of apostle, but he chose these men as a statement of God's transforming power.

Trust of Jesus

> *Greater love has no one than this, that he lay down his life for his friends. You are my friends if you do what I command. I no longer call you servants, because a servant does not know his master's business. Instead, I have called you friends, for everything*

that I learned from my Father I have made known to you (John 15:13-15).

Even though the disciples showed no apparent responsiveness to his teachings, as Jesus did with all men, "he *entrusted* himself to him who judges justly"[18] and poured out his love, knowledge and life for them. If Jesus' entrustment to the disciples was contingent upon the disciples' entrustment to him, we would still be lost today. Entrustment is trusting with no guaranteed return! Jesus was totally reliant on God's judgment of the Twelve. "I tell you the truth, anyone who has faith in me will do what I have been doing. He will do even greater things than these, because I am going to the Father."[19] Jesus not only believed that they could do what he could do, but even more. What entrustment and vision!

Even while he was dying on the cross, he trusted in God that the Twelve would eventually get it. Jesus went to the cross as a seemingly failed rabbi who had to trust in God's promise. What turned these men around to becoming world evangelists? Even after the cross, they went back to their old life of fishing. What happened?

Chapter

5

The Apostles' Response

Early in the morning, Jesus stood on the shore, but the disciples did not realize that it was Jesus. He called out to them, "Friends, haven't you any fish?" "No," they answered. He said, "Throw your net on the right side of the boat and you will find some." When they did, they were unable to haul the net in because of the large number of fish. Then the disciple whom Jesus loved said to Peter, "It is the Lord!" As soon as Simon Peter heard him say, "It is the Lord," he wrapped his outer garment around him (for he had taken it off) and jumped into the water (John 21:4-7).

What a sad sight. Jesus was raised from the dead, and he stood on the shore and saw a pathetic picture of his eleven disciples wallowing in self-pity in a fishing boat with no fish. When Jesus called out to them, they again caught a net full of fish, like the first time in Luke 5. Jesus had prepared breakfast for the brothers, and Peter was the first to jump out of the boat and reach Jesus. Peter probably did this out of a real joy of seeing him alive, but also from his guilt of having denied him three times.

When they had finished eating, Jesus said to Simon Peter, "Simon son of John, do you truly love me more than these?" "Yes, Lord," he said, "you know that I love you." Jesus said, "Feed my lambs." Again Jesus said, "Simon son of John, do you truly love me?" He answered, "Yes, Lord, you know that I love you." Jesus said, "Take care of my sheep." The third time he said to him, "Simon son of John, do you love me?" Peter was hurt because Jesus asked him the third time, "Do you love me?" He said, "Lord, you know all things; you know that I love you." Jesus said, "Feed my sheep.

    I tell you the truth, when you were younger you dressed yourself and went where you wanted; but when you are old you will stretch out your hands, and someone else will dress you and lead you where you do not want to go." Jesus said this to indicate the kind of death by which Peter would glorify God. Then he said to him, "Follow me!" Peter turned and saw that the disciple whom Jesus loved was following them. (This was the one who had leaned back against Jesus at the supper and had said, "Lord, who is going to betray you?") When Peter saw him, he asked, "Lord, what about him?" Jesus answered, "If I want him to remain alive until I return, what is that to you? You must follow me" (John 21:15-21).

Jesus did not forget Peter's lack of "followership" and called him back to his original calling in Mark 1: "Come, follow me." We can be all together and having a good time eating, but the "elephant in the room" must be addressed. Jesus did not overlook Peter's lack of leadership either, and questioned Peter about their friendship (*phileo* —verb form of friendship love). Peter felt really hurt by this, but true friends (Christians) keep their word, and he had not. Peter felt picked on by Jesus and tried to deflect the blame by asking a question about John. Jesus went on to restore Peter, and the others overheard this conversation. Sometimes in our churches, we make friendship and position more important than following Jesus, and this only causes dysfunction.

    In Mark's account, we see all the apostles scolded for their lack of followership. "Later Jesus appeared to the Eleven as they were eating; he rebuked them for their lack of faith and their stubborn refusal to believe those who had seen him after he had risen."[20] What happened to these men that they went from being misfits to world missionaries? I believe that these men were cut to the heart by the longsuffering grace of God. The kindness of Christ was overwhelming to them. Jesus loved them after their desertion, and this love brought about repentance and restoration. Jesus' love was clear in that he was still seeking to entrust and empower—for God disciplines those whom he loves.[21] They realized that they had been forgiven a lot, so they loved a lot. Consequently, these men turned the world upside down. Once again, we are reminded of Romans 2:4: "Do you show contempt for the riches of his kindness, tolerance and patience, not realizing that God's kindness leads you toward repentance?"

Jesus broke these deserters, liars and fallaways with his patience and love. Love brought them to their knees (a *baguette moment*). Who would make breakfast for eleven people who had left them and lied to them? Who would say "friend" to the one who had betrayed them? Who would pour themselves out for someone who did not deserve it in the least? Who would trust God and go to the cross, not knowing if these men would carry on their mission? Truly, Jesus embodied entrustment at its finest.

Many people are also misinformed about what patience really is. Jesus used patience with a purpose. Patience with no purpose is avoidance. Jesus used many real-life situations to show the apostles where they were spiritually.[22] Jesus patiently worked to develop Peter's character with a blend of stern discipline and encouragement, as one notices in Matthew 16:13-22. Jesus had an intentional lifestyle ministry. And his actions would resonate in the hearts and minds of the apostles for years after his ascension. Even though Jesus showed amazing patience, he still walked with his disciples. A common fallacy is the notion that people can change without a plan of repentance. Peter was told to feed his sheep and to follow Jesus. Jesus knew that if people are left to themselves without an intentional plan, their budding faith will eventually wither and die.

The brother of Jesus speaks on the principle, that true love involves action:

> *Suppose a brother or sister is without clothes and daily food. If one of you says to him, "Go, I wish you well; keep warm*

and well fed," but does nothing about his physical needs, what good is it? In the same way, faith by itself, if it is not accompanied by action, is dead. But someone will say, "You have faith; I have deeds." Show me your faith without deeds, and I will show you my faith by what I do (James 2:15-18).

James states that to only talk about helping those in spiritual or physical need, yet not seeing the need through to the end, is a lack love and faith. In churches today, many mask their inaction and neglect under the guise of being patient, or even being prayerful! The reality is that this can be cowardice if we aren't willing to love someone enough to confront their sin and see it through to the end.

Kindness costs. It costs something to care. There is often suffering involved on the part of the caregiver.

It is the kind physician who lances the boil, drains off the poison, cleanses the wound, and so restores the patient.[23]

Love is action. Who has the courage to lance the boil and stay in for the long haul and make sure all the poison is drained? The above quote by Keller reminds one of the Parable of the Good Samaritan (Luke 10), where we see two who only talked the talk (the Levite and the Priest–both very religious), while only one walked the walk (the Samaritan—despised by the Jews, but praised by Jesus). I would not let a friend sit in a burning building and not scream out and attempt to rescue them. We see many steeped in sin and lukewarm behavior,[24] but we often look the other way or look for someone else to intervene. God calls all of us to see the needs of others and to act!

See to it, brothers and sisters, that none of you has a sinful, unbelieving heart that turns away from the living God. But encourage one another daily, as long as it is called Today, so that none of you may be hardened by sin's deceitfulness (Hebrews 3:12-13, TNIV).

It is the responsibility of all of us to see that everyone does well. The Hebrew writer makes it clear that we must deal with sin at the heart level. Sin should not be full-blown before we act. When sin becomes full-blown, it also can contaminate others because of our lack of love to deal with it at the root.[25] Love always protects. One day of being in sin is too long, according to the Apostle Paul:

> *Therefore each of you must put off falsehood and speak truthfully to his neighbor, for we are all members of one body. "In your anger do not sin": Do not let the sun go down while you are still angry and do not give the devil a foothold* (Ephesians 4:25-27).

Jesus loved Peter enough to tell him the truth, and he quickly dealt with the deceitfulness of his heart that caused him to turn away from God. We must be proactive and not let Satan get a foothold in anyone's heart.

After the reunion and rebuke, he instructed his disciples to go back to Jerusalem and wait for the Holy Spirit there.[26] He had earlier promised to send them the Spirit and even described in some detail what the Spirit was going to do with them and for them.

Jesus Is Not With You, But In You!

I added this section after "finishing" the book and I truly believed that God held back the book because my thesis was not complete. It is obvious that the disciples were oblivious to the meta-narrative of God. After three years of walking, eating, sleeping and serving with Jesus, they still had no clue of what his mission was. In John 13-14, we find a pivotal passage that describes the Last Supper and the fear the disciples had of him leaving. Many questions were asked of Jesus about where he was going and if they could come too. Thomas said "show us the Father," so that they could believe. All the questions were of a physical nature and not spiritual. One reassuring statement from Jesus was "I will not leave you as orphans." Many who are faithful sometimes feel that God has left them all alone without a purpose or guidance. I believe that Jesus saw the fear and sense of "lostness" the apostles had, and he sees ours as well. Jesus reassured them and us with these promises from John 14:

- Do not let your hearts be trouble or be afraid (verses 1, 27).
- Trust in God and me (verse 2).
- There is a place for you (verse 3).
- I will come back for you (verse 3).
- I am the way, and the truth and the life (verse 6).
- You can do what I have been doing (verse 12).
- Do even greater things (verse 12).
- Ask anything in my name, and I will do it (verse 14).
- The Father is giving you a counselor (verse 16).
- I will not leave you like orphans (verse 18).
- He lives with you and in you (verse 17).
- I live, you live (verse 19).
- You are in me, and I am in you (verse 20).
- He who loves me will be loved by the father (verses 21, 23).

After this extensive reassurance, Judas (not Iscariot) made his gospel debut and asked Jesus again, "Can we come with you!" Jesus replied that the Counselor (the Holy Spirit) would come and remind them of what he had said during his time with them. The Holy Spirit would be in them and enable them to do greater things with the Spirit than even with Jesus being there in person. Why is that? Jesus realized that he was limited to one place in the flesh, but through the indwelling of the Holy Spirit,[27] they would never be alone and would also be empowered. Jesus stated that he had to leave in order for the Counselor to come and to guide them into all truth.[28] No matter where they went, even to the ends of the earth, he would be with them—no longer orphans and no need to be fearful.

Through the Holy Spirit and their obedience,[29] the dots would connect and the connection between the physical and spiritual would be plain and always true. In the mist of the disciples' insecurities, Jesus announced his entrustment of his Spirit:

- The world will not see me anymore, but you will see me (John 14:19).
- On that day you will understand unity (John 14:20).
- When the counselor comes he will teach you all things (John 14:26).
- I have told you this, so that when the time comes you will remember (John 16:4).
- He will guide you in all truth (John 16:13).
- The Spirit will take what is mine and make it known to you (John 16:15).

The Holy Spirit is the missing link between our flesh and spirit. Jesus' example, ministry, and even the cross meant very little until the Holy Spirit revealed God's eternal plan for all. Through the Holy Spirit the disciples were enlightened to see Jesus' purpose and were convicted.

Personal Note: Jesus has left all of us the ultimate tool of empowerment: The Holy Spirit who contains all truth, and is a Counselor who reminds us of all things (and a lot more than we can imagine!).

They Got It!

Now, Jesus' conviction, longsuffering patience and overwhelming love shown on the cross made absolute sense. Everything clicked, leaving no more duplicity or carnal thought. Now these fallaways were inspired by Jesus' life and love, the resurrection and the Holy Spirit, who produced in these men convictions that changed the world.

They stayed in Jerusalem and grew the church. For the Great Commission[30] to be fulfilled, Stephen was the sacrificial lamb (through the Holy Spirit) whose death scattered the church, so that the gospel spread outward from Jerusalem. These men were fearless and all were willing to die for Jesus. Someone's convictions are shown not only in the way they live but also in the way they die. Let's examine what was said about Jesus while he was dying on the cross:

> *And when Jesus had cried out again in a loud voice, he gave up his spirit.... When the centurion and those with him who were guarding Jesus saw the earthquake and all that had happened, they were terrified, and exclaimed, "Surely he was the Son of God!"* (Matthew 17:50, 54).

Hardened Roman soldiers on the crucifixion detail had watched hundreds of gruesome deaths, but Jesus' death was a divine moment. The apostles went from being apathetic to ambassadors, from deserters to martyrs because of Jesus' life of entrustment. Here is an account of some of their deaths.

James: The Brother of John

James who was in the inner circle of the three closest disciples to Jesus (Peter, John and James), was the first to forfeit his life. Shortly before his own death, King Herod (Agrippa I) arrested some disciples who belonged to the Jerusalem church and he had James put to death with the sword (Acts 12:1-2).

Peter: The Coward

Peter refused to die in the same position as Christ, asking to be crucified upside down. He died a martyrs death in Rome, circa 67 A.D.[31]

Paul: The Pharisee

Paul, the apostle, who before was called Saul, after his great travail and unspeakable labors in promoting the Gospel of Christ, suffered also in this first persecution under Nero...the soldiers came and led him out of the city to the place of execution, where he, after his prayers were made, gave his neck to the sword.[32]

Thomas: The Death of a Doubter

St. Isidore of Seville's testimony about Thomas:

"This Thomas preached the Gospel of Christ to the Parthians, the Medes, the Persians, the Hyrcanians and the Bactrians, and to the Indians of the Oriental region and penetrating the innermost regions and sealing his preaching by his passion he died transfixed with a lance at Calamina, a city of India, and there was buried with honor."[33]

James: The Brother of Jesus

He was elected to the oversight of the churches of Jerusalem; and was the author of the Epistle ascribed to James in the sacred canon. At the age of ninety-four he was beat and stoned by the Jews; and finally had his brains dashed out with a fuller's club.[34]

What changed these men was entrustment; Jesus trusted in God and poured himself out to this ragtag bunch, and the payoff through the Holy Spirit changed the world. His example was burned into their hearts and they followed to the bloody end. They got it—do you?!

Chapter

6

The Full Circle
of Entrustment

Paul and His Son!

> *You then, my son, be strong in the grace that is in Christ
> Jesus. And the things you have heard me say in the presence of
> many witnesses **entrust** to reliable men who will also be qualified
> to teach others (2 Timothy 2:1-2).*

Can we find Jesus' entrustment values in the apostle's
teachings? One of the most popular examples of entrustment was
that of Paul with Timothy. Timothy was referred to as a son by Paul.
They had a unique relationship, as shown in this passage:

> *I hope in the Lord Jesus to send Timothy to you soon, that
> I also may be cheered when I receive news about you. I have no
> one else like him, who takes a genuine interest in your welfare*
> (Philippians 2:19-20).

This passage describes the intimacy that comes with entrustment.
Where there is entrustment, there typically is a deep relationship.
Paul could not empower if there was mistrust. In contrast, Paul could
not initially work with Mark because he felt him to be unreliable.[35]
We must entrust the mission to reliable people[36] and "entrusters" must
possess a good judgment of character when it comes to leadership

ability. Paul was serious about the mission and of having committed individuals with him. We must protect the integrity of leadership and not succumb to sentimentality. Timothy, though young, stayed with Paul through his toughest times in Antioch, Iconium and Lystra, showing his loyalty through times of persecution. No wonder Paul wanted Timothy there with him in his final days.[37]

When the church in Corinth was riddled with sexual sin, lawsuits and divisions, and Paul had to eventually leave to allow the madness to calm down, he trusted Timothy to go in and reason with the church and be a key part in turning the church around. Timothy was also sent into Thessalonica after a riot. While Paul was in prison, one would imagine the churches might die out or greatly suffer, but through his empowerment strategy, the churches continued to thrive. Paul sent at least two letters to Timothy to help him with the church in Ephesus. In Paul's letters, we see the emphasis on entrustment. Timothy was charged as an evangelist to "discharge all the duties of [his] ministry." He was directed to appoint deacons and elders to share the load. Timothy had to entrust his duties to others for the collective health of the church. Paul's words in these letters describe his own calling, which he passed on to Timothy:

> *That conforms to the glorious gospel of the blessed God, which he **entrusted** to me* (1 Timothy 1:11).

> *That is why I am suffering as I am. Yet I am not ashamed, because I know whom I have believed, and am convinced that he is able to guard what I have **entrusted** to him for that day* (2 Timothy 1:12).

> *Timothy, guard what has been **entrusted** to your care. Turn away from godless chatter and the opposing ideas of what is falsely called knowledge"* (1Timothy 6:20).

> *Guard the good deposit that was **entrusted** to you—guard it with the help of the Holy Spirit who lives in us* (2 Timothy 1:14).

Paul Built All His Ministries on Entrustment

Though Paul did not spend time with the earthly Jesus as the other apostles did, he adopted his spirit and ministry model:

> By the grace God has given me, I laid a foundation as an expert builder, and someone else is building on it. But each one should be careful how he builds. For no one can lay any foundation other than the one already laid, which is Jesus Christ (1 Corinthians 3:10-11).

Through Paul's thirty years of ministry, he empowered and raised up Timothy, Silas, Apollos, Philemon, Jude, Titus and many more. Paul had an eye for leadership potential and character, but not every leader leads in the right direction, so Paul also had his disappointments in leaders such as Demas.[38] Leaders have free will too!

In Paul's letters, we see God's heart of entrustment passed on to the churches in Rome:

> Much in every way! First of all, they have been **entrusted** with the very words of God (Romans 3:2).

> But thanks be to God that, though you used to be slaves to sin, you wholeheartedly obeyed the form of teaching to which you were **entrusted**. You have been set free from sin and have become slaves to righteousness (Romans 6:17-18).

Paul's Words of Entrustment to Titus

> Paul, a servant of God and an apostle of Jesus Christ for the faith of God's elect and the knowledge of the truth that leads to godliness—a faith and knowledge resting on the hope of eternal life, which God, who does not lie, promised before the beginning of time, and at his appointed season he brought his word to light through the preaching **entrusted** to me by the command of God

our Savior. To Titus, my true son in our common faith: Grace and peace from God the Father and Christ Jesus our Savior. The reason I left you in Crete was that you might straighten out what was left unfinished and appoint elders in every town, as I directed you. An elder must be blameless, the husband of but one wife, a man whose children believe and are not open to the charge of being wild and disobedient. Since an overseer is **entrusted** *with God's work, he must be blameless—not overbearing, not quick-tempered, not given to drunkenness, not violent, not pursuing dishonest gain* (Titus 1:5-10).*

Paul reminded Titus of being entrusted by God to lead the church in Crete. He gave him some general guidelines, but he trusted Titus to appoint and empower an eldership to meet the holistic needs of the church. Leaders must pass entrustment on to keep the church functioning and thriving.

Paul to the Thessalonians

The church in Thessalonica is a true model of entrustment. Paul spent a few weeks strengthening the church and then due to severe persecution he had to leave.[39] He wrote about the church and stated that "he was afraid that the temper had got the best of them and their work was useless."[40] He sent in Timothy to see if his fears were true, but through God's grace and through Paul's ministry entrustment the church was faithful and joyful in affliction. If you left today would your situation stand the test of affliction? Paul knew that Satan wanted to destroy the church and started the empowering training as soon as he arrived in Thessalonica, not knowing what tomorrow might bring.[41] The true test of any man's work is what happens when they leave! Paul exhorted the Thessalonians with these words of entrustment:

For the appeal we make does not spring from error or impure motives, nor are we trying to trick you. On the contrary, we speak as men approved by God to be entrusted with the gospel.

We are not trying to please men but God, who tests our hearts (1 Thessalonians 2:3-4).

If Paul had not had Jesus' Spirit, the church would have crumbled because of ineffective and untrained leadership. Paul's legacy inspired and empowered later church leaders and theologians such as Polycarp, Tertullian and Justin Martyr.

In 64 A.D., Paul knew his thirty year ministry was quickly coming to a close. He left us a passage of Scripture that encapsulates the spirit and passion of empowerment, entrustment, loyalty and love. Here are some of the last written words of the Apostle Paul to his son Timothy whilst waiting to be brutally decapitated (the Roman form of capital punishment for its citizens) at the hands of Nero (these words brought me to tears):

> *You [Timothy], however, know all about my teaching, my way of life, my purpose, faith, patience, love, endurance, persecutions, sufferings—what kinds of things happened to me in Antioch, Iconium and Lystra, the persecutions I endured. Yet the Lord rescued me from all of them. In fact, everyone who wants to live a godly life in Christ Jesus will be persecuted... But as for you, continue in what you have learned and have become convinced of, because you know those from whom you learned it, and how from infancy you have known the holy Scriptures, which are able to make you wise for salvation through faith in Christ Jesus* (2 Timothy 3:10-15).

The Apostles' Ministry of Entrustment

Peter and John

The Apostles were exhorted by Jesus to fulfill the Great Commission:

> *He said to them: "It is not for you to know the times or dates the Father has set by his own authority. But you will receive*

power when the Holy Spirit comes on you; and you will be my
witnesses in Jerusalem, and in all Judea and Samaria, and to the
ends of the earth." After he said this, he was taken up before their
very eyes, and a cloud hid him from their sight (Acts 1:7-9).

Five years had passed since the ascension of Christ and his
apostles were still in Jerusalem! The scattering happened soon after
the death of Stephen.[42] The church was dispersed, and Philip found
himself in Samaria, whose inhabitants were historically hated by the
Jews. Even John (who later became known as the Apostle of Love)
had wanted to call down fire on a Samaritan town because they would
not allow Jesus to come through their city on his way to Jerusalem.[43]
Philip was a waiter for widows,[44] a relative "nobody" who would later
do something that even the apostles did not do—take the message to
Samaria. I believe that when John came out to assess the situation, it
was to see if the Samaritans could really be saved! He was so inspired
that he himself preached the word to the Samaritans as well! What a
transformation—Peter and John were empowered and inspired by the
work of the Holy Spirit in Samaria! When you are a true entruster,
you must step aside to make way for those whom God is using and
not hinder the Word and the Holy Spirit. John and Peter, pillars of
the church, assisted Philip's work through the Holy Spirit.

The Apostles

After Paul's conversion, instead of going to Jerusalem to see
the apostles, the Spirit empowered him to go straight to Arabia and
Damascus for three years![45] Paul finally made it to Jerusalem and the
Apostles heard what the Holy Spirit was doing in Paul's ministry. As
a result, they wrote a letter commissioning Paul and Barnabas to get
this message out to the Gentile churches:

It seemed good to the Holy Spirit and to us not to burden
you with anything beyond the following requirements: You are to
abstain from food sacrificed to idols, from blood, from the meat of
strangled animals and from sexual immorality. You will do well
to avoid these things (Acts 15:28-29).

The Apostles did not want to stifle the churches or micro-manage them; they trusted in the Holy Spirit.

When you see these accounts of Jesus' apostles, it becomes obvious that they were not held hostage by tradition, politics or "old boys' networks," but they were flexible and totally trusted in others to do the Lord's work. This happened because they entrusted themselves to the Holy Spirit more than to the personnel. After all, Philip was a deacon and Paul a relatively recent convert. Today, too many leaders look for those with seminary degrees and years of experience before they feel good about someone being in the ministry or going to a mission field. This means that they place very little emphasis on the Holy Spirit and what God is doing outside of their own sphere of influence. They often down play or minimize any good news from those who are not considered *chosen* by the hierarchy. This mindset will stop the growth of God's church and asphyxiate the Spirit's work. Yet, it is a mindset all too common in most religious circles. Many churches will not hire any staff person who has less than a Master's degree in theology. (Incidentally, I have a religious Master's degree, but I don't discount anyone who doesn't.) The apostles did not hinder the future of the church in such ways, and thus took the good news to Jerusalem, Judea, Samaria and the ends of the earth, fulfilling this Scripture: "I tell you the truth, anyone who has faith in me will do what I have been doing. He will do even greater things than these, because I am going to the Father."[46]

Chapter

7

Entrustment in Leadership

"We have to practice strictest daily discipline; only so can the flesh learn the painful lesson that it has no rights of its own."[47]

Jesus was a leader who entrusted himself to others. He poured himself out for individuals who often did not respond positively, but he kept on loving and training them. Today, we see many "one-man shows" in church leadership, unlike the model that Jesus has left for us. Many leaders talk about raising up the leaders of tomorrow, but they are not stepping aside to allow those new, young leaders room to rise up. Many call themselves leaders, but have no concept of how to train and empower the young.

The acid test for all preachers in the pulpit is how you share with the potential leaders of tomorrow. The next three chapters will highlight some universal principals that are hurting the empowerment process in churches of all types. My theological training has taken place in three different institutions: one would be considered quite liberal; another would be seen as quite conservative; and the third would fall somewhere in between. Therefore, what I say in this chapter has been developed by knowing ministers of all religious persuasions and practices, and seeing how their leadership played out in their congregations. In the critiques I give, I am not trying to produce negative attitudes, but I am trying to expose negative attitudes or approaches that are already present—for the purpose of helping all of us examine our ministries and ministry effectiveness. The goal is simply to help us all become leaders like Jesus.

One-Man Shows

The longer we deny the benefits of team leadership, the less likely it is that we will experience the power of God in the church, in society, or in our personal efforts. There is only one ministry superstar: Jesus Christ. If we persist in seeking to lead churches throughout the display of talents and abilities resident within only a few unusually capable individuals, rather than allowing the community of believers to use their significant-but-less-inclusive leadership skills in an orchestrated unison to accomplish synergistic outcomes, the church and society will pay the price for such defiance.[48]

In Texas, where I have lived for the last eight years, we have many one-man shows. Many ministers have split away from their denominations and gone out on their own. Some of them believe they had a sincere calling, but others who did not feel particularly led to do this simply wanted to have their own church. Characteristics of a one-man show include: one person being in ultimate control, lack of objectivity or oversight by other senior ministers and selectivity regarding who they allow to speak. It does not cross these ministers' minds that they could be a detriment to their own church. If only they would step aside and raise up others, they would be able to see that it is more beneficial to "their" church! Many congregants perpetuate this problem by stating, "I go to "Pastor Jim's church," as if he has in some way superseded Christ's ownership of the church.

Rob Bell described the trap of being a superstar when his church had reached 4,000. He fell in love with the honor and notoriety of being among the popular "mega ministers." Rob described his heart during this time as being on the "dark side" and having "no soul." Though he was preaching to the masses, he questioned if he was even a Christian (a *baguette moment* for sure)! Rob's situation is not uncommon, but it is rarely so openly expressed. Rob's fears and isolation caused him to go through the motions, and he "faked it" to thousands of his church members.[49]

Make no mistake about it—pastors are hurting others but also hurting themselves.

Hurting Pastors: They are pressured by the responsibilities of their position and are under the assault of the enemy. Some of their common concerns: 97% of pastors feel inadequately trained, 80% say their ministry has had a negative impact on their children, 70% struggle with depression,71% are having financial difficulty, 65% have thought recently about giving up on ministry, and 70% say they do not have a close friend.[50]

Fakers cannot train, and fakers cannot entrust because they have nothing inside to give. Are we still doing the same religious stuff that we did twenty years ago, even using the same old stories and leaving the progressive and creative Spirit of God outside the church? Many ministers and leaders will get frustrated in reading this book, assuming it is an academic program, but it is all about what is inside your heart and whether or not you really trust God and others. Personally, I don't care how big "your church" is or how long you have had *your church*. The thinking underlying this type of speech will steal your soul.

Another sign of being a one-man show is being unwilling to give up the "pulpit of power." The one-man show minister limits others because of his own insecurities. The excuse for many ministers is that there is no one out there to train! They are looking for people who think like them and have their same worldview, but those types may be hard to find. Remember that Jesus took assassins and tax collectors to train, and changed the world! We are without excuse! The power is in God's Word and through his Spirit, and we are all imperfect conduits. Remember, there is mistrust, trust and entrust, and entrusting is the only way to keep the church generational and growing.

Many hire from outside their local church, and this can

discourage internal advancement. Raising up from within will not only inspire others in the congregation, it will eventually create a synergy of young ministers and potential church leaders. When hiring from the outside, you are inviting in a stranger whose religious beliefs you may know little to nothing about. People might initially have more respect for someone hired from the outside, there must be support from the senior minister and from the congregation, so you can raise up home grown ministers from within your own pews. The opinion leaders of the church must be trained to let younger leaders lead them, which ensures a relevant and vibrant church for tomorrow. We sometimes forget that it took someone having enough belief in us to give us the freedom to make mistakes and to find our own homiletic footing.

Many older ministers deceive themselves into thinking that they are entrusters, but they were essentially forced to pass on the leadership torch because of necessity due to retirement, failing health or abilities. If the spirit of entrustment had been there throughout their senior ministry lives, there would be several protégés leading ministries around the world. It is sad to see many churches with declining attendance and mostly older members due to the lack of youth in the pulpit. Over time, these churches often die a natural death.[51]

Program-Driven Church

Examples of programs are age-graded Sunday schools, adult education classes, small-group ministries, need-based seminars or highly structured discipleship programs.

All of these programs can contribute to discipleship development, but they miss the central ingredient in discipleship. Each disciple is a unique individual who grows at a rate particular to him or her. Unless disciples receive personal attention so that their particular growth needs are addressed in a way that calls them to die to self and live fully in Christ, a disciple will not be made.[52]

Jesus commands intimate one-on-one relational ministry, which was the cornerstone of Christianity:

A new command I give you: Love one another. As I have loved you, so you must love one another. By this all men will know that you are my disciples, if you love one another (John 13:33-34).

Many churches have gotten away from walking one-on-one with people and have turned more to communal programs, classes, seminars, conferences and other events. I know of one church in the Dallas area that has sixty classes ranging in topics offered from how to study the Bible to marital issues. Seminaries teach classroom scenarios and not relational discipleship. Larger churches tend to offer classes for virtually any life situation their members might face. Their new members go through four to six introductory classes and still walk out confused about their true belief systems.

Classes can be a good tool, but they can never replace "one anotherness." A large majority of churchgoers go to church and have no interaction with their brethren outside of Sunday, making intimate fellowship virtually impossible.[53] The lack of intimacy will have a profound effect on people being open about their weaknesses and personal confession of sin,[54] something that can never be accomplished in an open class setting. Many use these classes as a *cop-out* to avoid dealing with their own life struggles.[55] Classes have a "shotgun" effect, where some are hit and others are missed. Whatever the case, the effects are shallow at best. Classes can stir the soul, but personal application comes with one-on-one intervention and accountability. Nathan personally had to confront David on his sin because David was self-deceived.[56]

Another spiritual discipline that is commonly an event rather than a lifestyle is evangelism—many wait for a campaign or a mission trip to share their faith. Another is serving the poor—some wait for a church-organized Thanksgiving Dinner or a Christmas toy drive to engage with the needy. One of my family's summer vacations was in Mexico. I had decided that one of our days of vacation would be devoted to the poor. We went to a local store and bought food, and our kids picked out toys and candy for the local kids. We headed out to the poorest part of town where the houses were made of corrugated tin and scraps of wood, with no electricity or running water. Giving in this way was so rewarding, and it made my kids appreciate what they have.

Many people want to make a serious one-on-one conversation only an event (an appointment), instead of making it a lifestyle. Also, many times we talk *about* people rather than talking *to* the ones about whom we are concerned. This is clearly a violation of what Jesus commanded in Matthew 18:15. I grew up as an alcoholic and I know the effects of addiction. Having a counseling degree and having spent hundreds of hours with addicts, I often found that many addiction groups become the addiction! Many use the group as a reason to be sober more than developing a reverent fear of God. Groups can work, but they must not be the ultimate reason for change. It must be God. We all must be held accountable by the omnipresence of God.[57]

Men and Church

In conclusion, this lack of focus on the entrustment process has had a profound effect on the male's perspective of the modern day church. It has often been said that men hate church.

> Today's church does not mesmerize men; it repels them. Just 35 percent of the men in the United States say they attend church weekly. In Europe male participation rates are much worse, in the neighborhood of 5 percent. This hardly sounds like a male-dominated, patriarchal institution to me. What's worse, nobody seems to care about the absence of men. Have you ever heard a sermon on the church's gender gap? I've never heard a pastor or church leader bring it up. Heck, I've never heard anybody bring it up. It's just one of those things Christians don't talk about.[58]

As leaders we must not be oblivious to what we see in the pews. According to Marrow, the Muslims, Buddhists and the Jews have a better man-to-woman ratio than Christianity has, and yet we are not alarmed! It starts by giving men a vision and helping them fulfill the dream that God has put on each man's heart for greatness.[59] Paul understood the future of the church, and thus shared (and even reduced) his apostolic power by empowering *men* such as Timothy, Titus, Silas, Apollos, Barnabas, Erastus, John Mark, Aquila and many others. Men feel alive when they are empowered!

Postmodern (Contemporary) Leadership—Some Solutions

Let us focus on some keys to turn the tide of male apathy and inadequate leadership in the church. One of these starts with not allowing youth ministers to become pigeon-holed in this role, because many leaders see them as only that—and have no other vision for them. In and outside the church, people are screaming for the leadership for tomorrow, but few senior ministers are empowering young leaders by making room for them at their side. Many one-man show ministers are insecure or do not have the ability to train others and thus are spiritual dead ends. Young leaders also have a challenge. They must want to be led; and in being raised up, they sometimes must do things differently than they would if they were in charge. (Remember: different does not mean compromising your convictions in Christ.) Only when both are fulfilling these challenging roles (the senior minister making room and the young minister humbly stepping up into that space) will the cycle of empowerment of new leaders take place. Jesus empowered the apostles, and after his resurrection, they changed the world.

There seems to be a great disparity between youth and adult ministry, and many leaders seem to feel that somehow this will change without anyone making an effort to cause the change. The chasm between generations can cause churches to split. Often, when the kids reach college age, they leave church for the world, leaving behind church traditions that are no longer relatable to them. In trying to attract and retain multiple demographic groups, some churches have several services to cater to the different worldviews. I believe that young leaders who are truly empowered can speak powerfully and persuasively to those of all ages. How can we really be "one church" otherwise?

I do believe the decline in church attendance is an indication that the traditional message is not connecting with this postmodern audience.[60] It is imperative to understand this principle and let the "postmoderners" use the pulpit to ensure a church for our children and grandchildren. I grew up in England, and I have personally seen what it is like to live in a country that is two generations removed from the Christian faith, where churches have been converted into bars and restaurants (See Appendix II). Explaining the process of empowerment will also help the protégé to understand the steps of entrustment. By training leaders to train others, we will ensure the future of the church. We must create an environment of empowerment by being willing to step away from the pulpit, always remembering that Jesus is the true "superstar."

Successful Preachers

Today, we have "Preachers" who deliver sermons without using the Bible!

> "We (ministers) think the Bible is too difficult, irrelevant, or just plain boring and if we use it, people will quit listening, as if they are going to be scandalized by the fact we have dared to open the Bible—in church of all places!" [61]

I will be candid with you. It is easier to preach or do something myself than to train someone else. It takes hours of listening, reasoning and repeating myself before someone I'm training understands the true spiritual principles of preaching. I have spent untold hours in my kid's room, having many a man preach at a podium made of my kids' toy containers. In this setting, I can critique not only the content of his message, but also his delivery, including his facial expressions and gestures. The supposed "best" seminar/class teachers fill the minds of fledgling ministers with theory, which will only have a limited impact, unless they are walked with, watched and critiqued through several sermons. Otherwise, it is only cognitive training and they are left lacking in the pulpit. Training takes time that some senior ministers are not willing to put in. Many preachers are "last-minute wonders," writing their sermons the night before they speak. These men barely have time for themselves, let alone time to train others!

> The supreme work of the Christian minister is the work of preaching. This is a day in which one of our great perils is that of doing a thousand little things to the neglect of the one thing, which is preaching.[62]

It takes time to develop a sound sermon, and it has taken me years to effectively develop this art (and it is an art). This is time well spent, but an equally important need is the training of others who have been called to preach and teach. If we neglect this, we are taking care of the pressing needs of the moment but not laying a foundation for the future. One must spend time in the trenches with the youth to be able to recognize potential leaders, and then to work with the young ministers to develop them. On a recent Sunday, we had a regular service with a twist, because every facet of the service was led by teens and those in their twenties. Some parts were more effective than others, but the buzz in the congregation afterwards and the thought of empowering and building for the future made up for any shortcomings.

I believe that for those of us in our forties and up, half our time must be spent training and empowering the leaders of tomorrow, creating a fertile ground for the Holy Spirit to work so that others can reach their full potential. A friend of mine, Sam Powell, once stated that "Success will be measured by one's successors!" Let's be successful!

J -Walking (Walking like Jesus)

As God has said: "I will live with them and walk among them, and I will be their God, and they will be my people" (2 Corinthians 6:16).

Jesus spent three years walking with, eating with and confiding in his disciples, but today's leadership paradigm usually consists only of weekly meetings, emails, text messages and a couple of phone calls. The apostles learned from watching Jesus with the people.[63] Their experience ranged from observing how Jesus served the poor to seeing him confront the Pharisees; thus his disciples learned how to deal with a plethora of problems and individuals.

Young men and women have aspirations for doing great things, but they are too often limited by their leaders' egos, lack of training abilities and insecurities. Many leaders don't trust their interns to have larger responsibilities and the interns are not being adequately trained. Youth ministers are being hired, and yet there is little or no "hands-on" training by walking with them and helping them with the basics of overall ministry. Interns in these situations are doomed to fail and those who should be their trainers are often the first to criticize their inabilities—even when they have failed to train them! We should not be surprised when interns leave the ministry disillusioned and go into a secular field. If you are training them to be a campus minister, then you should be on campus with them, providing the needed on-the-job training.

J-walking with someone exposes the teacher's life and personal example. It is difficult to train others when the teacher lacks respect for the young person's calling, and ends up acting only as a figurehead with no substance. Leaders cannot rest on their past reputations assuming that they have already "arrived." This only deters them from walking with the very people they are supposed to be leading and training.

> *We loved you so much that we were delighted to share with you not only the gospel of God but our lives as well, because you had become so dear to us* (1 Thessalonians 2:8).

According to this passage, it takes love to share our whole life. I try to be transparent and open my life up to others. I have most of my appointments in my office in my home, and people see how my kids act, they see my marriage dynamic with my wife and they see the way I live with no attempt to hide anything. Ministers who always want to meet with others away from their homes (usually in a church office) miss the opportunity to demonstrate what is going on in their homes. This is like saying I want to be a superstar without the paparazzi. But being like Christ means opening one's life up to others. We must be opening our homes and practicing hospitality, seeking input on how to be a better parent or spouse—even from those we are training. There have been times when my wife and I have gotten into a disagreement in front of people and then asked for input to learn from what they perceived in our interaction. Jesus walked along with others as he taught and spoke the truth to them. J-walking is a way of life—the Jesus' way of life.

He walked and talked truth. It was not an event—it was just a way of life. Community programs are fine, but we must have personal intervention with the hurting, the deceived, the poor and the lost.[64] Christ-likeness describes who we are and not what we do! "To this you were called, because Christ suffered for you, leaving you an example, that you should follow in his steps."[65]

Paul adopted this J-walking principle. It is evident in one of the most endearing statements of Paul's love and entrustment, as he commissioned Titus to go into Corinth (one of the most challenging of ministry situations): "We (Titus and I) have the same spirit and walk in each other's steps, doing things the same way."[66] Walking is an organic process and not sterile, limited, or corporate. This type of leadership is relational and intimate. It works, and no other approach does. We simply must become convinced of this principle of leading and training at the same time.

Here is one relation empowerment story: Jason

Jason was a very effective youth minister, who at age 30 was married with two children, and was making the transition into the adult ministry. He was uniquely positioned to make this transition, and at the same time, refresh our adult ministry and make it more attractive to younger members.

We sat down to make a development plan. Phase One was to get the congregation to view him as an adult minister. His worldview had to change from teens to adults. His preaching lacked depth and insight. We came up with a plan to raise up others to take over the youth ministry. We started off slowly and planned for him to begin leading a small group of adults, and to alternate with me in preaching every other week. Jason's preaching quickly improved, and some months he preached more than I did! Every time he spoke, he became more relatable to an adult audience. After every sermon, there was a detailed critique and discussion. He has gotten to the point where he is using cutting edge audio/ visual aids which I have never used before and he brings a postmodern message mature enough for the adults, and one that will also relate to the youth, who are the future of the church.

He and I have spent many hours talking about different situations in his group. The next stage in his transition is to assume responsibility for a ministry of 100-plus adults, and eventually to be raised up as a church leader. For these adults to feel secure in the transition, they must feel that Jason will be able to relate to them and will meet their needs. He has been set up for success through training, developing his spiritual giftedness and his faith in God. He has thrived throughout this empowering process, which has taken a year up to this point. Without total entrustment, Jason would have felt like a fill-in or an assistant, and this would have hindered his true potential in Christ.

My Personal Stories of Entrustment

I have had many people influence my life. I remember one occasion when I was only a few days in the faith. A minister (Thomas) took me under his wing and walked with me. He was also pivotal in helping me come to faith. He also baptized me. Within a few weeks, he had me lead my first Bible discussion group. I was fearful but felt empowered. I used a prop in my discussion and I thought it went well! I'm sure Thomas could have found much fault in my lesson, but he just encouraged me to preach the Word. After his encouragement, I felt like I could walk on water! A few weeks later he left, due to some personal issues, and there was no one qualified to lead our group. Due to his training and entrustment, I felt called to pick up the ball and run with it. When the upper leadership found out that our group was "leaderless" but saw that God was working through our fledgling group, I became our leader by default!

Another personal empowerment story is about my first time to preach. I was so zealous and excited. Three of us were given the Great Commission as a lesson topic; I spoke on "Go make disciples." I came up with an idea on making a disciple like making a cake, and used a creative "recipe" to make a disciple. Another minister (Dave) sat down with all of us and went through our ideas and reasoned with me to tone down my illustration. I was so excited that he suggested that I should color code my lesson: green for calm, blue for normal and red for "let it rip!" The direction and colors helped me to deliver my first sermon. Dave stepped away from the pulpit and empowered three "young guns" to preach. This exposure awoke the desire for me to become a preacher and aspire for the ministry. Through these minister's examples and more like them, I have been able to pass on God's entrustment to others. You can find some of their personal testimonies in Chapter Ten.

"Everyone leaves a legacy, whether you have children or not." We all influence the people we encounter. If we want to leave a godly legacy, we will need to live for God's glory, teach God's ways and confess our sins (to each other).[67]

Interestingly, as I write this very chapter, I am being empowered by an older, experienced writer and close personal friend, Gordon. He offered to help me put the finishing touches on my book, which led us to spend three days together (what a sacrifice). He is trying hard to walk the fine line of offering editing suggestions without interfering with my content or my way of communicating it. In other words, he trusts me enough to entrust me with his expertise, knowing that I will pass on what I am learning to others who want to write.

In conclusion, brothers and sisters, we should not let our insecurities, egos, lack of forward-thinking, lack of transparency or our inexperience in the trenches hinder the Holy Spirit from changing and using us. There are too many people who want to do great things for God for us not to be entrusters. Again I end with the last words of the imprisoned Apostle Paul to his friend and successor:

You [Timothy], however, know all about my teaching, my way of life, my purpose, faith, patience, love, endurance, persecutions, sufferings—what kinds of things happened to me in Antioch, Iconium and Lystra, the persecutions I endured.... But as for you, continue in what you have learned and have become convinced of, because you know those from whom you learned it, and how from infancy you have known the holy Scriptures, which are able to make you wise for salvation through faith in Christ Jesus (2 Timothy 3:10-15).

Part Three

Domestic Entrustment

Chapter

8

Entrusting in Parenting

Jesus continued: "There was a man who had two sons. The younger one said to his father, "Father, give me my share of the estate." So he divided his property between them. Not long after that, the younger son got together all he had, set off for a distant country and there squandered his wealth in wild living. After he had spent everything, there was a severe famine in that whole country, and he began to be in need. So he went and hired himself out to a citizen of that country, who sent him to his fields to feed pigs. He longed to fill his stomach with the pods that the pigs were eating, but no one gave him anything.

When he came to his senses, he said, "How many of my father's hired men have food to spare, and here I am starving to death: I will set out and go back to my father and say to him: Father, I have sinned against heaven and against you. I am no longer worthy to be called your son; make me like one of your hired men."

So he got up and went to his father. But while he was still a long way off, his father saw him and was filled with compassion for him; he ran to his son, threw his arms around him and kissed him.

The son said to him, "Father, I have sinned against heaven and against you. I am no longer worthy to be called your son." But the father said to his servants, 'Quick! Bring the best robe and put it on him. Put a ring on his finger and sandals on his feet. Bring the fattened calf and kill it. Let's have a feast and celebrate. For this son of mine was dead and is alive again; he was lost and is found." So they began to celebrate.

Meanwhile, the older son was in the field. When he came near the house, he heard music and dancing. So he called one of the servants and asked him what was going on. "Your brother has come," he replied, "and your father has killed the fattened calf because he has him back safe and sound."

The older brother became angry and refused to go in. So his father went out and pleaded with him. But he answered his father, "Look! All these years I've been slaving for you and never disobeyed your orders. Yet you never gave me even a young goat so I could celebrate with my friends. But when this son of yours who has squandered your property with prostitutes comes home, you kill the fattened calf for him!"

"My son," the father said, "you are always with me, and everything I have is yours. But we had to celebrate and be glad, because this brother of yours was dead and is alive again; he was lost and is found" (Luke 15:11–32).

I started this chapter with the story of the Prodigal Son to show how parenting challenges are timeless. Even today, it takes all the energy and determination my wife and I have to instill character in our kids without exasperating them.[68] Parenting must be intentional, and it must seek to develop Christ in the child.

I remember after each of our children were born that we prayed in the delivery room. We thanked God for our child and vowed that we would do everything in our power to get his child back to him. Holland and Segovia are loaned to us to teach us to be like Jesus so that we can do the same for them. When our children were at the early age of 18 months, we started to curtail the emotional tantrums, and we instilled within our kids the principle of first-time obedience by the time they were two. Obedience and respect for authority are the ABC's of parenting and discipleship, especially if they are going to learn to obey God's Word and respect those teaching it. Without these principles in place, you will have no trust or change.

As our children grew, we realized how different they were from each other. Segovia is the extrovert, and my son Holland is more of an introvert. Our children are so different from each other that we must adopt separate character plans to form Christ in them.

We often speak of making disciples of Jesus[69] to describe our heart for the lost, but this same principle applies to our kids. Many churches have classes or a study series to help people become disciples. The challenge I have for the parents is: are you making disciples of those around you (especially your children), dealing with the signs of rebellion and repentance? We can become out of touch with the process of seeing Christ being formed in others, and therefore are not skilled in discerning this process in our kids. By the time our kids become teens, we should be trained in disciple making, and this training should be evident in the lives of our own family. If you are not making disciples of those outside your family, how can you make disciples of your family? I believe that God's plan for salvation is flawless if we are daily walking like Christ.

There is no better tool for instilling these values than the parent's own example. I heard once that parenting is 80% *caught* and 20% *taught*. What will turn off a child is to teach them correct behavior and insist that they follow rules that you are not living by. The most impressionable years of a child's life are spent watching their parents; and this can be either good or bad. Many want the youth ministry to convert their kids, teach them to read their Bible and share their faith. By age thirteen, these things should be what the child is accustomed to seeing at home and not a foreign concept.

Prodigal Principles

There comes a time in parenting that our children have to find themselves and form their own worldview on what is right or wrong. Many of our kids are going to make the right choices and live fruitful lives in Christ, but there are those who want to test what is true by venturing out to explore the world and themselves. When you experience friction in every conversation with your child and they are not respecting you, many call it rebellion. Although there is truth in that description, it is also a time when the adolescent is fighting for his own independence and establishing his own belief system. It can be a most painful time, and parents can feel powerless when they see their little "baby" do things that are contrary to what they believe. But this must be allowed to run its course, a point I touched on early in this book. A parent must pray and hope that what they have instilled in their children will bring them back to God.

When it comes to developing Christ in our children, the Bible has a great example of free will and parent/child dynamics. In Luke 15, we the familiar story of the youngest son who wanted his independence, and took his inheritance and left home. The father was hurt by the decision, but he let his son go then waited until he came to his senses and returned home. The younger son left in arrogance, but he came back grateful, humble and loving. The father did not chase after his son, but waited in love instead. According to Jewish law, because his son had defied his father's wishes, the Jewish community had every right to kill this rebellious kid:

> *If a man has a stubborn and rebellious son who does not obey his father and mother and will not listen to them when they discipline him, his father and mother shall take hold of him and bring him to the elders at the gate of his town. They shall say to the elders, "This son of ours is stubborn and rebellious. He will not obey us. He is a profligate and a drunkard." Then all the men of his town shall stone him to death. You must purge the evil from among you. All Israel will hear of it and be afraid* (Deuteronomy 21:18-21).

This son's actions could have cost him not only his inheritance, but also his life. Even the dad said that by leaving, his son was as good as dead, as we see in this passage: "But we had to celebrate and be glad, because this brother of yours was dead and is alive again; he was lost and is found."[70]

In every prodigal story, we see the same principles of

entrustment, one must know when to let go and trust in God's processes in our child's life. Our children must have their free will, and they must taste death and come back to a new life in Christ. Parents who coddle their kids and do not have the patience to watch their kids go through this process, may well end up with an older son who is obedient (sometimes through people pleasing) but full of resentment because they have lived their parent's life and not their own. As parents, we walk a thin line between having a rebellious child or a people-pleasing child. Godly parenting is not an easy task!

Signs of a Prodigal Mind

Flee the evil desires of youth, and pursue righteousness, faith, love and peace, along with those who call on the Lord out of a pure heart. Don't have anything to do with foolish and stupid arguments, because you know they produce quarrels. And the Lord's servant must not quarrel; instead, he must be kind to everyone, able to teach, not resentful. Those who oppose him he must gently instruct, in the hope that God will grant them repentance leading them to a knowledge of the truth, and that they will come to their senses and escape from the trap of the devil, who has taken them captive to do his will (2 Timothy 2:22-26).

I start off with a caution when it comes to figuring out the prodigal way of thinking: Don't! A prodigal mind, according to Jesus, is a person who has lost their senses, and psycho-analyzing their actions and words will only send you to therapy! Many parents want to fix or solve this cognitive labyrinth, and they end up getting frustrated and often give up on their child.[71] Remember this: how can you understand someone who doesn't understand themselves? The mindset of a prodigal is self-centeredness and irrational thinking. Even in the case of the Prodigal Son, he asked for his inheritance —which is normally given to a child after the parent is dead! The audacity to ask for it when your father is alive puts in jeopardy all the father has worked for. What was he thinking? Obviously, he wasn't thinking! The best strategy with prodigals is to exercise patience and prayer in hopes that they will "come to their senses" and realize their ways are harmful to themselves, God and others.

Many prodigals are deceived and believe that they can make it on their own. They don't listen to advice and most have an independent spirit. These kids must find out that there is more to life than the character-debilitating coddling and the thinking that is done for them at home. But, they must be put into situations while still under your roof where they will be humbled and realize that life is tough and they don't have all the answers. A prodigal must always be helped to stay in touch with their shortcomings and inadequacies. This will keep them grounded and nourish a sense that they need others. But do not exasperate them; pick your battles carefully. This preemptive parenting requires recognizing the signs of "prodigalism" early, thus saving a lot of strife in the family. The signs include an escalating resistance to your direction, shallow dialog, not sharing what's going on in their lives, having peers and role models outside the home and the church, constantly making poor choices and a reluctance to participate in family activities.

Many parents are oblivious to when their child has crossed the line and shut down emotionally toward them, and when that point is reached, every word they are saying is pushing that child further into the "free will-derness." The same principle of being oblivious applies when the parents themselves have crossed the line and continue to push their child to the point of exasperation. Once the prodigal has made up their mind to go, any advice will only exacerbate the situation and could postpone their return. This is really where most of the damage is done with prodigal children, leaving everyone in a stalemate. A wise parent will see the fruitlessness of arguing and debating, change their strategy and prepare to send the prodigal out in love. Remember, the most lasting thing that they should feel is your love and that they are always welcomed back.

One strategy is not to continue try to persuade them to stay, but rather to reason with them about where they are going. Many prodigals hate where they are, but they have not evaluated where they are going! Thus they go from the frying pan into the fire! This line of reasoning can be effective. It will plant seeds that will help bring about "right thinking" more quickly; your words might resonate as their life deteriorates. Another strategy is using their friends to reason with them and try to persuade them to evaluate their decisions. If your child has reached this point, you are playing catch-up at best, and preemptive parenting is the best strategy. The great inspirational passage for parents who are in this situation is found in Romans 12:12: "Be joyful in hope, patient in affliction, and faithful in prayer."

Will-derness Survival

The son in our story had probably learned to work hard from working on his father's land, and while he was away, he ended up working with pigs. As parents, we must do whatever it takes to set our kids up for spiritual survival in the free "will-derness." Teaching them to cook (I learned at 10), to cleanup after themselves, to get themselves to school, to earn their allowance, to work a part-time job—this is how we will foster strong character in them. Ultimately, building a child's character must be at the forefront of every parent's mind. You must show them that you trust them, and empower their thinking to make decisions and accept the consequences of those decisions. Many kids cannot think for themselves and are paralyzed by life challenges because their parents have done all their thinking for them. Many parents are more aware of developing their child's educational résumé than in developing their character and their spiritual survival skills for the will-derness. Teach them how to multi-task—I have witnessed numerous parents who have only had their children focus on just academics while at home. Once off to college they have academics, a job, financial responsibilities, domestic duties, general life stresses (choices) and oh, yes, don't forget to be righteous! This is a major learning curve which could be overwhelming to an unsuspecting teen. Prepare your child for life's will-derness!

The Prodigal eventually realized that he had sinned, not only against his father, but against heaven as well. We must listen to our kids as hard times affect them. Some whine and complain about their circumstances, but they have not connected it to God. Seeing our kids suffer is one of the most heart-wrenching experiences a parent can have. We must stay strong and endure watching them suffer until they turn back to God. Being in the will-derness can make you prayerful. Even as a non-believer stranded in Europe with "a baguette and a can of Coke," I prayed! The will-derness can break down the hardest atheistic heart, and parental sentimentality will only hinder God's process. I am living proof of this principle. Sometimes, your child needs several *baguette moments* to come to their senses.

Many parents get so frustrated that they make the kind of statements that can leave long-term scars and are very difficult to repair—statements such as, "Get out and never come back," or, "You are not my child," or, "I wish I never had you," or, "If you hang out with them, you are not welcome in this house." Kids who hear these things from their parents can feel so rejected that they can never come back. Controlling, threatening parents who heap guilt on their children will have a devastating effect on them.

Preemptive Parenting

The media promotes the notion that parents are idiots and that the child knows best. (Satan always tries to totally reverse God's truths.) Cartoons such as Jimmy Neutron the "kid genius", Johnny Test and many other kid /teen programs are *anti-parent*. My wife and I once went to the movies and saw a scene where two kids (age six to ten) beat an adult while speaking in a derogatory way. I have seen an increased use of these types of scenes to get a cheap laugh, but it sends a message to the kids that it is acceptable to be physically and verbally abusive to parents and others in authority. You must watch what your child is watching, explain to them how these shows are demeaning to others, and help the whole family develop clear expectations and set appropriate boundaries.

An early sign of a child's waywardness is who their friends are, for these are their main influences.[72] Knowing this, boundaries must be set up, guided by this principle: *You hope for the best and prepare for the worst.* Many parents set up boundaries too late, after communication has totally broken down, and the boundary setting comes across as controlling and full of ultimatums. It is better to state these rules prematurely than to wait until it is too late and the situation is out of hand.

You must keep rules clear and simple. Have only three or four rules, and set them early before the sin becomes full blown.[73] Here is an example: (1) Come home before midnight; (2) When at home with another person from outside the home, keep the door open; and (3) Have a weekly parent/child time. Discuss what the consequences should be for disobeying the rules and work this out together. There should be no surprises. The open-door policy will promote friends coming over, and with light supervision, it should create a fun environment. I would rather have my daughter in my home with her boyfriend (supervised) than with him in the back of a car in a dark parking lot! Have an open home and maintain a fun environment with reasonable boundaries. This might mean buying a cool X-Box and a big-screen television! Understand this: I am not into materialism, but I am into doing what it takes to save my child. Be cool parents. Prodigals tend to demonize their parents to their friends. Be hospitable and warm, and you might be surprised how God can work in the hearts of your children's friends. Go out of your way to love those whom your child loves and those with whom they associate.

Your one-hour, weekly time together will be an opportunity for you and your child to connect and touch base. Say 'no' to distractions and 'yes' to real dialog. Family meals will be an opportunity to bring up any family issues and resolutions. What child would not agree with just two hours a week out of their schedule to be with their parents? To make this a family tradition, start it early and do not sway from it. For the last several years, we have committed every Monday night to a family meal together; we also play games (which have exposed sibling rivalry) or watch a movie at that time.

These prodigal boundaries are there to protect the other siblings too. The other kids are watching and will only become resentful if there are different rules for them when they come of age (like the older son in the prodigal story). Explain to them what is happening, and pray with them for their sibling. Use any prodigal event to show the devastation of sin and how this kind of life is empty. These conversations must be done in love and not in a cynical or demeaning spirit against the wayward sibling. Obviously, if your child's behavior is so extreme that it is affecting the other kids or your marriage, then hard but loving decisions have to be made. A conversation must be had to reaffirm the communal rules, and based on these rules (which were agreed to by both parties), we may have no choice but to make other arrangements for where they live. Even in this extreme situation, all this is still done with a warm demonstration of love. The prodigal should not be surprised; they probably know what is coming. Today, in our churches and society, it has become the norm to be overly concerned with what the minority feels (the prodigal in this case), but sentimentally pleasing one person is never of greater importance than saving the whole family.[74]

Once you know you have tried all your preemptive measures and your child decides to still leave for the will-derness, a final act of love would be to throw a going-away party and help them move! Have a time of sharing memories and stories of love, and during this time, share hope for their return and assure them that the door is always open. If you are reading this and going through a "prodigal moment",[75] you may be angry and confused. The father in the prodigal story still gave his youngest son his inheritance, though he knew that his son had lost his bearings and that he would eventually blow it on wild living! The father did whatever he could to set his son up for success, without imposing on his free will. Please do not take this as encouragement for enabling addictive behavior; for example, if your child has a history of substance abuse, I would not advise you to give them money.

This reverse thinking will take emotional and spiritual maturity if you are to come across as sincere.[76] The ones closest to us sometimes hurt us the most, and even if your child seems like your enemy, here are some words of encouragement: "If your enemy is hungry, give him food to eat; if he is thirsty, give him water to drink. In doing this, you will heap burning coals on his head, and the LORD will reward you."[77]

Love will win in the end! This time of sharing is not a time to co-sign for their sin, but to reconfirm love and hope.[78] In many situations, hurtful words have been said and everyone involved is hurt. As a parent, this is a time to forgive, to resolve grievances in your own heart and simply love your child.[79] Your child has lost their senses, and you are the older and more mature person spiritually. Therefore, you must rise above the hurt and love your child. Paul called the Christians in Asia Minor to remember Jesus during a time of turmoil in His life:

> *To this you were called, because Christ suffered for you, leaving you an example, that you should follow in his steps. "He committed no sin, and no deceit was found in his mouth." When they hurled their insults at him, he did not retaliate; when he suffered, he made no threats. Instead, he **entrusted** himself to him who judges justly. He himself bore our sins in his body on the tree, so that we might die to sins and live for righteousness; by his wounds you have been healed* (1 Peter 2:21-24).

We entrust ourselves to Christ and the Cross and not to man. We are called to sacrifice, even when insulted and hurt. Always remember, love never fails.

Living by the Law or the Spirit

Many parents try to impose Christian rules and conduct on their pagan teenage kids, wanting them to pray, read their Bibles and go to church against their wills. Trying to enforce Christian values on pagan kids is a disaster in the making. Many make the statement, "As long as you're in my house, you are coming to church!" This can give rise in the teenager to resent their parents, God and spiritual practices. We have a cousin who, at age eighteen, has been told by her parents that she must go to a church on Sunday and not stay in bed. She goes to church because it is required, and she gets very little out of it. Now, since leaving home she has not gone to church! Many who have this type of upbringing are hesitant once they leave home to come back to church, because of the religious charade they have been required to perform. Act according to your convictions, but don't impose it on others. Be limber and loving. Some children leave you no choice except to have them with you due to their immaturity, but this need for extra supervision should be explained to them.

Families may have the advance understanding with their children that a part of family tradition is attending church on Sundays together. However, this should be explained clearly when the child is younger and receptive for if it is done later when in the middle of their "prodigal moment" this will come across as an ultimatum. This is a part of what we called earlier "preemptive parenting," and is clearly different from issuing ultimatums. Free will is an empowering tool God gives us to build character, gratitude, humility and brokenness. Once we have exercised our *free will,* we can freely and without reservation or regret come to do God's will. Combining freedom with wise parenting gives the child the best shot at making good decisions.

Are You Ready to Run?

When the father saw his son a long way off, he ran out to get him. This may have been to protect his son from the townsfolk; to show them that he loved his son and that no harm should be done to him. "Filled with compassion,"[80] the father put himself in the shoes of his son and overlooked the rebellion. The joy of the dad is amazing in this story, and the connection between the two is stronger than ever. Their relationship is now organic, not based on authority, guilt or need. This son has become a man of God. God let his child go, and so must you. Not letting the child go will create a battle of wills and a long-term rift between parent and child. It will breed a lack of gratitude and character development. Many times, kids will become deceitful because they do not want to disappoint you and because they fear your overreaction to their honest feelings.

The father ran to his son because he saw him turn back. A parent must be alert and look for signs of their prodigal turning to God, and then must run out. We must be patient, but when they turn back, you had better be ready to run. Many parents miss opportunities to instill spiritual convictions in their children because of being emotional and spiritually overwhelmed or disconnected. Discouragement can keep us navel gazing and feeling sorry for ourselves, rather than looking out for our child's return. Resentment and religious embarrassment can cause us to minimize any changes in our child and miss ideal moments to intercede. Sarcasm will only shut down openness and hinder the child's return. A prodigal situation can happen in the home without them ever leaving physically. When dialog is down to grunts or full-out arguments, the whole family feels the emotional rift. At this point, they have already left home in their hearts.

The father in the parable kept looking out for his son because he had never lost hope for his return. Today, many parents are working to keep their kids in a "good" home and a distinguished school district. We are so overwhelmed with our bills, maintaining too much house, our children's sports activities and homework that we are not watching out for our kids' spiritual development. The father was watching for his son to turn back to God. He did not hesitate. He probably had his slippers on, and would have made quite a scene running down the road in his dressing gown to embrace and protect his son.

Love Never Fails

Along with the child's free will, there must be parental love. Love is truth. Telling your child, "I don't agree with your actions, but no matter what happens, I will still love you," sends the right message to your child. Do not exacerbate the situation, but do watch for burnout and be alert to your child asking for input. Unsolicited input may fall on deaf ears, but be ready to run when they are asking for spiritual help. Many teens feel if they do not do exactly what their parents demand, their parents will not love them. It is painful to be estranged from those you love. Assure your children that, even as they always have their free will, they also always have your love. The prodigal son knew that he could always come back home. Build a home of love and be patient, and chances are much better that they will come back![81]

Children and Their Changing Attitude toward Their Parents

Age 4:　"My parents can do anything."
Age 8:　"There might be one or two things they don't know."
Age 12: "Naturally, my parents don't understand."
Age 14: "I never realized how hopelessly old fashioned they are."
Age 21: "You would expect them to feel that way; they are out of date."
Age 25: "They come up with a good idea now and then."
Age 30: "I wonder what Mom and Dad think I should do?"
Age 40: "Let's be patient until we discuss it with our parents."
Age 50: "What would Mom and Dad have thought about it?"
Age 60: "I wish I could talk it over with them one more time."[82]

A Little Assignment

If you have the time, download a song by Taylor Dayne called, *Love Will Bring You Back*. If you can listen to this song (at least three times) and not cry while reflecting on God's love for you, your spouse and your wayward child, I will personally refund your iTunes fees! Here are some of the lyrics, written by Diane Warren:

> *But I know in time*
> *That we'll be together*
> *Oh, I won't try*
> *To stop you now from leaving*
> *Cause in my heart I know.*
> *(chorus)*
> *Love will lead you back*
> *Someday I just know that*
> *Love will lead you back to my arms*
> *Where you belong*
> *I'm sure, sure as stars are shining*
> *One day you will find me again*
> *It won't be long*
> *One of these days*
> *Our love will lead you back*

While listening to this song, imagine a loving father or mother looking out for their son or daughter from a distance, ready to come running out and embracing their homeward child. Love will bring them back.

Warning To All Prodigals: You Think It's Bad Now!

All prodigals feel that they know better than those around them and honestly feel that they are better off leaving. The reality is that many leave with their self-centered convictions and come back convicted. The prodigal son left with his inheritance and came back broke. He left with some faith and came back unclean and unholy. He left pursuing freedom but came back enslaved by sin and shame. When leaving home he thought he was "living the life" but came back spiritually dead. There is no free lunch with prodigalism and there can be lasting consequences. The Jews had strict purity laws and you have to wonder who would marry this man after he had been with prostitutes. The rift between him and his brother would take months or years to mend; he came back a mere shadow of the man he was when he left. God can forgive your sin, but we are left with the scars! Sin always leaves its mark.

Personally, I reflect on other *baguette moments* (I have enough to open up a French bakery) where in my wildest dreams I could not imagine myself behaving in such a way. One time, I remember collapsing in drunken stupor in my grandmother's spare room and waking up in my own vomit! Also, I remember waking up with women whose names I did not even know and had no idea how I got there! My fraternizing and abuse of women reach a defining point when a girlfriend came at me with a knife—yes, a knife! She wanted to kill me and I saved myself by wrestling the knife out of her hand and holding her down for close to an hour until she calmed down! Another *baguette moment* occurred just before Bob and I were separated in Amsterdam. We were waiting to purchase some drugs to sell in another country! While waiting for the pick-up, we were involved in a scary high speed chase with the Dutch police through Amsterdam. I was just a boy from Norwich, England, who left home to have a little fun and to find myself! This *fun* turned into women wielding knives, drinking binges, homelessness and then selling drugs (and I didn't even smoke cigarettes)! The deception of sin will paint a picture of freedom and the ultimate utopia, but this is far from the truth. What starts out as a dream usually turns into an absolute nightmare!

> *Children, obey your parents in the Lord, for this is right.*
> *"Honor your father and mother"—which is the first commandment*
> *with a promise— "that it may go well with you and that you may*
> *enjoy long life on the earth"* (Ephesians 6:1-3).

The reality is that there are some universal truths in life. If you are not at peace with your parents, your past, yourself and God, don't expect things to go well for you. If you are leaving home, do everything in your power to first be reconciled to your family and then go in peace. I left home and moved 5,000 miles away with domestic unrest at home and with deep inner turmoil inside me. You can go 5,000 or 10,000 miles away, but you take yourself with you and all of your baggage and baguettes too!

Chapter

9

Entrusting in Marriage

Marriage means...
Two imperfect mates
Building permanently
Giving Totally
In Partnership with a perfect God.
Marriage, my love, means us![83]

I have been married for eighteen years, and I feel that I am still learning to love my wife as Christ loves the church. The thought of a woman committing her life to me is overwhelming. My wife has been a faithful and spiritual mainstay in my life and has always supported me, even when I was not thinking rationally! She has always trusted in God that I would come to my senses and make the right call. Marriage is a wonderful structure in which one can learn how to take care of another. Once you get married, you must consider your spouse before making decisions. This can be a challenge for those who have been single for awhile.

Marriage must be built on Trust

Love is patient, love is kind. It does not envy, it does not boast, it is not proud. It is not rude, it is not self-seeking, it is not

easily angered, it keeps no record of wrongs.
Love does not delight in evil but rejoices with the truth.
It always protects, always trusts, always hopes, always perseveres.
Love never fails (1 Corinthians 13:4–8).

Love always trusts. If one is going to have an entrusting marriage, it starts with trust. You cannot say "I love my spouse" without truly trusting them. Many go into marriage with dysfunction, perpetuated by poor role models and personal sin. Many get caught up in the idyllic image of marriage and do not realize that marriage is all about two sinners becoming one! There have been periods in our marriage where we have "hit the wall!" One of these *baguette* times occurred about five years into our marriage. Things had gotten so bad that my wife did not want to talk to me anymore, and she meant it! I was a young minister and didn't want our superiors to know about my neglect, or about the discord in our home. During this time, our home had become a battleground of mistrust and thinking the worst of each other. We were combatants and competitive with everything, from correcting each other's diction to disputing about which one was working the hardest. The peace and trust of Christ had left our home. My wife felt that I was not listening to her needs, and in turn, became more condescending. She became angry and felt unappreciated by me for all that she did around the house.

I was hurt too, because I was taking care of the bills, shopping and cleaning up the house. I felt as though asking a third party to come in and help us in our marriage would be like throwing myself to the wolves. No doubt Ephesians 5 and the husband's responsibility to lead his wife would be used as a club to beat me over the head! I already *knew* she was wrong and I was going to prove it! I was desperate, and through heated debate, we decided to go to the Bible to prove who was right. I was going to study all the passages about husbands and she would study all the passages about wives; then we would come back to discuss our findings. Yes, I was going to prove that she was a bad wife, biblically! I even envisioned her crawling in submission[84] to her husband, who after all, is called the *stronger* vessel in the marriage![85]

As I studied, my smug self-righteousness turned to soberness. It dawned on me that I had fallen short in my love for my wife and that I did not trust her heart to change. When we came back together, we listened to each other, and all we could do was to apologize to one another! From that moment on, we decided to appreciate every little thing we each did for the other, and this created an affirming atmosphere of gratitude, which we maintain to this day. My wife and I are opinionated people, and we know that without God, we would be divorced.

As a husband, I was not empowering my wife. I was beating her down and being critical of all the things she was *not* doing, instead of appreciating all the changes that she had made. What convicted me the most was that I did not trust her heart. My wife's intention is to please me and ultimately God. I took my eyes off her heart and looked at her actions, where we will all fall short. I can overlook an offense if my wife is, in her heart, striving to be like Christ.[86] When I started to trust my wife's heart, she began to flourish and became radiant.[87] The specks disappeared and she became someone without a blemish and holy in my sight. (She was already that in God's sight —Ephesians 5:27). When we stopped being competitive and critical, the empowerment process began. Our marriage became a safe place where I could be open with my feelings and we could pray together about hurts and weaknesses. I still find it hard to apologize quickly, but I am getting there.

Everett L. Worthington Jr. states, "When a person feels supported and secure, when the person feels valued, conflict triggers can be ignored. The partner can brush off the conflict instead of pulling the trigger." We put our emotional guns down and our house became the "Okay Corral," with less shoot-outs! When my wife and I trusted each other's hearts, we stopped tearing one another down. We started to entrust each other, and in our marriage, and we have never looked back. Thank you, Jesus!

Sharisse: An Empowered Wife's Testimony

Marvin and I have been married for eighteen years. In and of itself, this is amazing. I did not grow up with a lot of healthy examples of marriage around me, much less, examples of mutual respect and trust. I am grateful that, truly by the grace of God, I am able to experience great emotional freedom and trust in my marriage.

I met Marvin when I was 18 years old. We met at a gym where he worked. Sadly, our initial attraction was based on "lust at first sight!" Needless to say, the premise of our relationship was purely physical. Unfortunately, this type of relationship was not founded on truth, but on superficiality!

This relationship quickly proved to be like every other relationship I had experienced with a man, always failing because its foundation lacked substance. When I was in my young, teenage years in search of love, I had been with quite a few untrustworthy men who certainly did not have my best interests in mind. And by the time I was 19, I had had my fill of these kinds of relationships and was desperate for something far better!

I was doing some modeling during this time in Los Angeles, when I had met an amazing model at a fashion show named Lisa who happened to be a Christian woman. We immediately hit it off. I was drawn to her spirit. Later, she invited me to her church which she was enthusiastic about. After several invitations, I finally attended. I was amazed by the fellowship and the deep sincerity of everyone wanting to truly walk as Jesus did.

Soon afterwards, Lisa encouraged me to study the Bible with her, and I began a wonderful journey. There were, however, some bumps along the way. Marvin, who was my boyfriend at the time, was an atheist. This posed a huge challenge to my faith, for God directs us in his word not to be yoked with unbelievers. I had a huge choice to make. A part of me wanted to ditch what I was learning in the Bible and just settle for what was comfortable and normal to me, but another part of me wanted to have a relationship that was built on something far more substantial than me!

Good news! God won, and I chose to surrender my life to him and get baptized. God helped me to relinquish my worldly relationship, and Marvin and I ended up breaking up. I was convinced that if God wanted me to be with Marvin, it would be because he would become a Christian man! So I extended an invitation to Marvin to come and check out church with me, and to even study the Bible just as I had. He begrudgingly accepted. I could, in no way, have imagined all that would transpire due to a simple invitation!

Marvin then began to study the Bible. He immediately started to develop a true faith in God, and he set about practically applying God's Word to his life. I was impressed by the rapid changes he was making for God in his life. A short time later, some bad news surfaced. As he was attempting to repent in certain areas of his life, he admitted to me that he had cheated on me during our two-year relationship. This was devastating. But what else should I have expected, given that our relationship was not based on the Rock.

What was encouraging is the fact that God was now re-creating our relationship based on his standards of purity and truth. God gave me the courage to forgive him. Marvin soon was baptized. We starting dating again (this time in purity) and six months later we were married.

Now, we have a beautiful marriage that is based on truth, honesty and fun. I know that because of our committed relationship to God, I can fully trust Marvin and he can trust me. Furthermore, because Marvin is striving to be a godly husband, he helps to bring the best out in me. I am able to walk about my life with great confidence and freedom.

A relationship built on Christ has empowered me to be a better woman, friend and mother. I feel the complete freedom to grow as a person, and Marvin has always been a huge support in that way. Case in point, when I was a child, I was sexually molested by my stepfather. This had a tremendous impact on me. Marvin gave me the support and space I needed to wrestle through my healing. I also embarked on managing depression in my life. He was extremely supportive as I explored counseling to get well. During this time, he took care of the whole family by cooking and taking care of all the chores. Lastly, I have decided to go back to school to earn my degree in counseling. My husband has fully empowered me to pursue this dream.

A lot of the things I've been able to do and explore would not have occurred had I not felt so empowered by God and my husband.

Though our lives are busy, we still have weekly lunches where we sit down and talk about our kids, marriage, finances and our relationship with God. What I really enjoy are our monthly date nights. I am so very grateful to God and my husband for allowing me to spread my wings and fly in so many areas of my life! I have had lots of strife in my early life and have shed many tears. But my tears today are tears of gratitude and laughter! Thank you, Lord.

Prodigal Husbands

In many marriages, there are husbands who do not believe, or who are lukewarm spiritually. Most churches have many more women members than men. This should not surprise us, considering what we read in the Gospels. After the death of Jesus, it was the women who were at the tomb. Eventually, after much persuasion,[88] Peter and one other disciple went to see if their Lord was resurrected. But for the most part, the men were in hiding behind a locked door![89] When Jesus appeared to them while they were eating (we men love our food!), he rebuked them for their "stubborn refusal" to believe that he had risen from the dead.[90] Women seem to have a more dependant spirit and they thrive in intimate communities, whereas men can be loners. Most men see that their job as family leaders is to provide for the physical needs of their family, and they are often oblivious to the emotional and spiritual aspects of family leadership. Prodigal husbands usually have a problem with their Christian wife tithing when finances are tight. These men like their wives to be Christians because it means they're not out with the wrong crowd and that they will be patient with them. Prodigal husbands use Christianity as a tool to their advantage.

Such men are usually overwhelmed with life, family and marriage. They may well have married when they were too young and have remained too immature. And despite the fact that it was lust at first sight, it seems like in a blink of an eye they have two kids and multiple responsibilities. The wife thought she could change him over time but actually things have only gotten worse.

Men, you have three choices in how to handle this scenario: (1) you can stay in your marriage but crawl into your *cave*; (2) you can leave your family, thinking there's a better life out there; or (3) you can decide to stay and grow. Real men always take choice #3.

Homebody

In family life, men by nature are ordinarily lazy and just want to be left alone. Many a man enjoys Sunday mornings when the wife and kids are at church, because it means he can watch the game in peace! These men do not have the energy to go out and act a fool! They sit on the couch and grunt, snort and complain. They get involved in pornography on the internet, chat rooms, excessive playing of video games and movies with explicit content. The wife does everything around the house and takes care of the kids. I imagine that it is hard to watch a husband deteriorate, when it is obvious that he is miserable and empty inside. For a woman in such a position, I say, you have to pray for a wakeup call, that he will hit rock bottom and come to his senses. Try to have small gatherings at the house and have Christian men connect with him by playing video games or engaging with him in his hobbies.

During the 1990s and 2000s, a common theme on sitcoms like *Roseanne* and *Everybody Loves Raymond* is showing wives disrespecting their husbands. Some husbands feel like derelicts because of the constant nagging of their wives, and they just shut down. Contrary to the message of these television shows, to get the best out your husband, believe and respect him, and let him know that you are his advocate.[91] Remind him that he is still your pumpkin pie!

I Was Her Pumpkin Pie

Before I married Maggie dear,
I was her pumpkin pie,
Her precious peach and honey boy,
The apple of her eye.
But after years of married life
This thought I pause to utter:
Those fancy names are now all gone,
I'm just her bread and butter.[92]

Flirting with the Edge!

Some husbands are living on a dangerous edge. They want their marriage and the thrill of the flirt too. These guys are social and have a lot of friends. This is probably one of the reasons his wife married him. Sometimes the reality of true married life cramps this man's style because he prefers the life with no responsibility and freestyle living.

I am a very social person too, but I must have boundaries, especially with the opposite sex. There are signs that things may have gone too far with another woman, like when your husband is having phone conversations secretly, not allowing you to look at mail or emails and not being able to account for blocks of time in his schedule. Having separate bank accounts shows a lack of trust and openness. Watch for who your husband's friends are, and if they are single and up to no good, remember: "Bad company corrupts good character."[93] Early interventions are the key. If you need to, have people reason with him and help him consider what he has to lose.

I recently came back from South America and met a faithful sister whose husband's actions were dubious to say the least, but she had no real evidence of unfaithfulness. Instead of pulling back and becoming mistrusting (she knew that this behavior could have an adverse effect and push him into another woman's arms), she loved her husband all the more! I was shocked. Then it dawned on me that her love could not be duplicated by any other woman. Although they might be younger or prettier or sexier, she was not going to be out-loved! She treated her husband like a king and served him. Sisters, when you are tapped into God's love, no women can replace that.[94] You are a daughter of God; you do not live or love by the standards of this world.[95] These infatuations will burn out and God's love will prevail. If you treat your husband like this he will think twice about chasing the flirt. The woman described above took the path of loving some sense into her husband!

Disclaimer: The *baguette* is baking! Some husbands must go on this fruitless pursuit to eventually come back like the Prodigal son—humble, broken and appreciative of who you (the wife) are and of the longsuffering love you have shown. You must weigh the cost of this decision and its impact on you and the kids—spiritually, emotionally and physically. (A great book for healthy marital parameters is called *Boundaries in Marriage* by Cloud and Townsend). Do not jump to conclusions and only work with the facts. Trust me; such a husband's folly will be exposed. Ding! *Baguettes*, anyone?

> *Every prudent man acts out of knowledge, but a fool exposes his folly* (Proverbs 13:16).

The Religious/Good Husband

Many men go to church, many have good morals and many take care of their families; and all of these must be commended. Yet, religious husbands can still be unconnected emotionally and spiritually with their spouse. Consequently, the wives are the spiritual leaders in the family, which contradicts Paul's exhortation in Ephesians 5:23. In such situations, the wives are the ones who initiate spiritual activities with the family, and the husband tags along for the religious ride. The kids see their dad being friendly, going to parent/teacher meetings and showing up for games, but there are no deep talks and no concern shown for the things of the heart. The heart is the essence of a person. You must go heart-to-heart to have true intimacy with your child or your wife. "Now that you have purified yourselves by obeying the truth so that you have sincere love for your brothers, love one another deeply, from the heart."[96]

God expects heart talk and constant connectivity; some men can hide behind their religious veneer and not get open and real. This type of prodigal husband minimizes and runs from intimacy. They avoid conflict[97] and if nagged by others will make a half-hearted effort but it's not their genuine conviction. Prodigalism is shown in this type of individual by running from one's emotional and spiritual responsibilities.

I have also seen certain religious men who can be detached one minute and when prompted (constantly nagged) they wake up and get hard line (even harsh). There's truth (even scripture) with no love![98] Due to their overreacting people in general feel not listened to or shut down. These husbands have no middle gears, they go from first to fifth, and then they go back to their cave of unconsciousness (first gear) and wait for their next prompting! This husband has two extreme personalities—oblivious or obtuse (harsh)!

My wife has helped me learn to express how I feel and how to be constantly connected especially with my kids. We must fight their sinful character to become like Christ, who lived a *life* full of gentleness, compassion and expressed himself through his feelings.

> *During the days of Jesus' life on earth, he offered up prayers and petitions with loud cries and tears to the one who could save him from death, and he was heard because of his reverent submission* (Hebrews 5:7).

Jesus expressed himself with tears and sincere emotion. What has happened to the GENTLE man? Have we forgotten what a real man should act like? Guys, our wives need us and our children need us to express affection and words of affirmation. Its okay, you won't die; try it! And when you do, watch them light up!

To the Prodigal Husband

(I know there are prodigal wives out there, but I want to speak to the husbands.)

> "The greatest thing a father can do for his children is to love their mother. And the greatest thing a mother can do for her children is to love their father."[99]

If you are a prodigal husband, I want to first commend you for reading this book. But I must also challenge you to get real and become grateful! Look at what your wife is doing and has done for you. Look at your kids and reflect on how your example will affect them. You are creating dysfunction that will affect generations to come.

It's time to come clean and get open. I know you are empty,

but you are too prideful to admit it. Stop the masquerade! Write a letter or a list of things that you are going to be open about, and be truthful. Write down how you are feeling about your marriage, your family and yourself—emotionally, spiritually and physically. Realize your own *baguette moment*! I have a song I want you to listen to when you have finished. The song is called, *Water Runs Dry* by Boys II Men. I have cried numerous times listening to this song, and Lord willing, it will move you, too. If it does not move you while you are looking over what you wrote, I will again offer to refund your iTunes fees!

The song is based on a couple who have slowly drifted apart. They communicate only through meaningless pleasantries and conflict. Both of them know that time is running out. They are in a stalemate. Please, listen to the song. It will change your heart.

Water Runs Dry

We don't even talk anymore
And we don't even know what we argue about
Don't even say I love you no more
Cause sayin' how we feel is no longer allowed
Some people will work things out
And some just don't know how to change
Chorus:
Let's don't wait till the water runs dry
We might watch our whole lives pass us by
Let's don't wait 'till the water runs dry
We'll make the biggest mistake of our lives
(Boys II Men 1994)

Being a prodigal husband is the biggest mistake that a man can make. It will affect your children and your children's children!

Take a moment to think of a man who is spiritual and has a great family and marriage; someone who you can set up a time with to pour out what really is going on in your life and heart. Ask for advice, and then heed it. Pick up the phone and call the man, set up a time and then start working on your letter.

Make the call now! The next chapter will be here tomorrow, but your somber spirit might not!

Recent research is shining light on the importance of male spiritual leadership in the home. Among their findings is the reality that 68 million of our nation's 94 million men don't attend any church. This, in spite of the fact, that 86% of them grew up with some sort of church background. Research has revealed that if a child is the first person in a household to become a Christian, there is a 3.5 percent probability that everyone else in the household will become Christians. Not very high at all. If the mother is the first to accept Christ, the percent goes up and 17 percent of the homes will see the remainder of its members trust Christ. But if the father is first, there is a 93 percent probability that everyone else in the household will follow. When father goes first spiritually, good things happen at home. Let's all pray together that God will call even more men to spiritual revival and renewal. Never has there been a generation in our nation where it is has been more important than now.[100]

Make the call!

Are You Really Surprised?

Many make a crucial mistake during the dating process. Young couples get caught up in lust and romanticism. Common sense is abandoned, supplanted by feelings as the guide to behavior. The relationship has no foundation of trust, integrity, character and self-control. Lust, emotion and rebellion take center stage. Marriages happen with no premarital counseling, leaving couples oblivious to the traps into which most relationships succumb. The husband then becomes a father and he is quickly in over his head. He lacks the intimacy skills and spiritual aptitude to lead a family, and he either shuts down or goes out to be free! Many, like me, lacked role models as a child, and are left to find direction on their own, often looking to the media and the streets for guidance.

Even those wives and husbands who see the signs of "prodigalism" during dating still ignore it, thinking it will change, or that they can "fix" their spouse over time. Maybe you saw the flirtatiousness, the laziness and immaturity, but you romanticized that there would be a perfect prince on the other side of the marriage altar, only to find that afterwards, to your *surprise*, it got worse! We made a vow to stay with each other through sickness and in health, in good times and bad. If you believe that we can get the best out of our spouses by nagging, making sarcastic remarks and bad-mouthing our spouse to the kids, you are painfully deceived! Much of our negative behavior toward a prodigal spouse is based on fear of what our lives together will be like in the future.

Sisters, men have *"moments"*! Every prideful man will have moments of humility and clarity. Their hard exterior is a thin veneer covering up tremendous insecurities and discouragement. Mistrust and nagging shuts a man down, but a patient, loving and entrusting wife will open them up. When these moments happen you must be spiritually and emotionally ready to draw your mate out. A wise wife will not overreact with anger and sarcasm but start building an open dialog. You must wait for the moment when the seemly impregnable veneer will crack or chip. Wait for that moment! Remember that patient love drives out fear.[101]

To give hope, here's a story that will help you stay the course to the end, no matter what!

"I'll Stay With You"

William and Mary Tanner were crossing a railroad track some years ago when Mary's foot slipped and became wedged between the rail and a wooden crosswalk. Frantically she tried to get loose as a train approached around the curve. Her husband attempted to free her. As the express came closer with its brakes screeching, Mary realized it couldn't stop in time. "Leave me, Bill! Leave me!" she cried. Seeing his efforts were useless, he arose quickly and held her in his arms to protect her as much as possible. While bystanders shuddered in horror, the train thundered over them. It was reported that just before the engine hit them, they heard the brave man cry, "I'll stay with you, Mary!"[102]

Oil to the Grind

In conclusion, sometimes life feels to me like one great corporation or a domestic production line. My life can be full of deadlines, meetings and kid's activities. Life becomes mundane and quite frankly, it grinds, which is no fun! If you are like me you need some oil! Many marriages deteriorate because they have devoted all their time and energy to their kids and employment but not to one another. You are actually harming your kids by putting them first, teaching them to put their kids and their jobs before their marriage and God (this produces generational dysfunction). Your kids must hear and see that your marriage comes before them and their relational and academic aspirations.

Most of our kids will be in the home between eighteen and twenty-two years, before or after college (if they go). I have a few questions: where will your marriage be when it just you and your spouse standing there in an empty house? There will be no sports or kid's events to distract you from your ailing marriage! What are you going to do? Are you more excited by *me* time than *our* time? What do you still have in common? Are you even friends? Where's the romance? At this stage of life, many only stare at each other as strangers! We have a close friend to whom we are reaching out, who has openly stated that when the kids leave she wants a divorce! Due to the years of neglect in her marriage, a relational chasm has formed which is irreconcilable in her mind.

It is time to stop the grind! Get back to what you did at first and what made you close in the beginning. It was the quality time together going on dates, the getaways, and the hobbies you both liked to do together. Become spontaneous again and start having the weekly times to talk and have intimate conversations without distractions. Have some fun! Yes, it's allowed in life. I'm giving you permission! Having these special times are the oil to life's grind. I know it is more challenging now with kids and more responsibilities but it will be worth it. Start with one thing and remember "A little water goes a long way in a parched desert!" Daily prayer (ours are nightly) and openness will keep you spiritually connected as a couple. Do the things you did at first and get that romance back. It's time to get the oil out!

Part Four

Testimonies
of Entrustment

Chapter
10

Testimonies of Entrustment

In my studies, I have read many books containing a lot of theory but very little practical application. To avoid this pitfall, I wanted to include real-life examples. Candidly, the testimonies I am including at this point create considerable uneasiness in me. I recall the passage in Proverbs 27:2, which states: "Let another praise you, and not your own mouth; someone else, and not your own lips." I decided, in spite of my own discomfort, to include them anyway, for two basic reasons: One, it will help make the point that I do practice the principles that I describe in the book rather than just espousing theories; and two, the testimonies will "flesh out" many of the specifics in the entrustment process of training others. Do keep in mind that I know I have not arrived at perfection in any of the areas I describe—I am a disciple, which means I am a learner on a journey. Frankly, I desire to become what Jeremy and Carlos already think I am!

Jeremy and Carlos have agreed to share their experiences and their perspectives on true entrustment.

Jeremy: My Testimony

I grew up in an interracial family, not fitting in with blacks or whites. I always felt like an outsider. I never knew my dad. My mother and I (and my sister) stayed with different relatives for several years. These uncertain times brought physical and emotional abuse in my life. Even at the age of five years old I was in counseling. Mistrust filled my heart and friends were hard to find. I came into the church looking for a safe haven and stability.

My past has been a constant battle for me while being in the church. When I was baptized in the Dallas church, I was fired up. I was quickly raised up and I found myself leading Bible discussions after a few weeks. God used me to see many come to Christ and be baptized. A couple of years later, the church was going through some challenging times and some of my close friends left the Lord. This revealed to me that my spirituality was dependant on man, more than God. I was living on other's convictions. I started to free-fall spiritually; this led to chronic impurity and eventually led me into sexual immorality with a stranger.

I moved to Wichita where I had a semi-spiritual revival but the deep rooted insecurities were still there. I developed a desire for ministry which led me to Los Angeles to a ministry internship program. God blessed my efforts and many were brought to the Lord. This success gave me the courage to return to Texas, but my insecurities and unresolved issues would soon be revealed!

I arrived with dreams and aspirations and soon I felt like a fish out of water, many of my childhood insecurities flooded back into my heart. I became prideful with the leaders and was eventually laid-off from my ministry job after 18 months. I left that ministry feeling like "damage goods!" I still believed that God was calling me to the ministry but I was imprisoned by my past! Many leaders said I should get out of the ministry. During this time I spent hours on the phone with Marvin (I had known him for four years at this point) and he would encourage me to trust in God.

Then a miracle happened and a ministry position opened up in Marvin's ministry in Dallas. God put me in a safe place to deal with some of my inner "demons!" Marvin understood my situation because he had experienced the same type of upbringing as a child. We spent many hours talking through my upbringing and spiritual formation.

I have been with Marvin for a year now and I describe this time in ministry as a "Journey to Freedom." I am free to express myself (the good and the bad) and he empowers me to be the best minister I can be for the Lord. God has given me much success as far as numerical growth here in Dallas but peace in my heart and mind is priceless. I have finally started to connect the dots between my past and my view of authority. My prodigalism manifests itself by failing to deal with my past. Instead of working on the inside, I would look at my ministry results for solace.

This freedom journey (It has not ended yet) reminds me of Jesus' interaction with a person in need: the story of the woman who was bleeding for twelve years. She was healed by touching Jesus but was not at peace. He called out "who touched me?"[103] I believe that he said this because if she would have left, she would have been healed but not at peace. Hence, Jesus' reassurance to her, "your faith has healed you. Go in *peace*."[104] For years I was healed but not at peace. God has finally brought some closure in my life and used Marvin and many others to bring about my healing.

Carlos: My Testimony

As a Christian, I've had my share of ups and downs. The Bible says in Ecclesiastes 7:14 that God gives us both good times and bad to help refine our characters. It is quite amusing that I prayed boldly to God saying, "God I want to go through the hard times first and then let the good times roll." Little did I know that God's answer was going to be, "Very well, it will be as you have asked!" The hard times did come at first as a little rain, and then as an outpouring of trials, adversity and difficulties that seemed to never end.

I was baptized on April 8, 1990. I had been in America for four years at that time, having come from Colombia (South America). I worked in many dead-end jobs, but I remained faithful to God, for he was my number one priority. It was my delight to be part of the church and lead different groups in hopes of being fruitful and helping other people to grow as well. One of my goals was to be in the ministry and I envisioned touching thousands of lives. As time went by, my initial joy and passionate zeal began to turn into criticalness. My faith turned into doubt, and I started to question God to the point of giving him ultimatums. I began to notice that despite my faithfulness to God, everyone else was being blessed with the things that I desired. I felt humiliated, forgotten, pushed aside and less than second best. It was then that bitterness and cynicism really took hold of me. I felt like the older son in the story of the Prodigal son. The convictions about righteousness and purity that I once held so dear became feeble and weak.

In 2001, I entered my very first dating relationship, but both of us were doing poorly spiritually. I wanted to marry this girl, but Marvin, who was my minister, refused to bless this union without extensive counseling and a personal spiritual revival from both of us. My resentment for him grew and he became the object of my wrath, for I believed that he was not supportive of me. Eventually, more sin came to light after some dear friends confronted me on my erratic behavior and secrecy. I was finally open about my immorality and sin with the sister I was dating. Marvin and the brothers sat down with me and they warned me about my sin; but I was hard-hearted.[105] Because of my continual sin, its deception, and my unrepentant heart even while many brothers were trying to reason with me, Marvin and the elders had to warn me publically. They encouraged me to read a general statement before the church to request prayers for my repentance.[106] I became even more resentful and my bitterness grew by leaps and bounds. Shortly afterward, I decided to move to a different part of the church since my resentment and hatred towards Marvin had become unbearable. I ended the relationship with this sister whom I had been so sure I wanted to marry! It was obvious at this point that I had only been trying to fuel my lust and cover my sin. I pray to this day that this sister will forgive me.

A few months later, I met another sister and I started dating her. Because I had not dealt with my heart, the same sin of sexual immorality followed me into this relationship. It was then that I decided to leave the church, rather than being asked to leave. I married this woman a few months later, and needless to say, it was a bad marriage from the beginning. I tried joining another church and seeking the help of counselors, but it was to no avail. Less than a year later, we were divorced. I continued visiting different churches for a while, but that did not last long. Eventually, I abandoned my faith and my convictions, and I started going out with women in the world in order to obtain a quick fix for the loneliness I was feeling. I had many one-night stands, but the emptiness and guilt of that lifestyle caught up with me. It was then that I started to cry out to God to be restored. And believe it or not, the hardest part of coming back to church was facing disciples, especially Marvin, all who knew that I had been publicly warned.

Through the help of some old friends and one of the elders, I started to attend church again. I had to wrestle in prayer to have the humility in my heart to face the man whom I once had despised so deeply. To be truly restored, I had to face my greatest fear: sitting down and talking with Marvin. We met at a restaurant and to my surprise, the time went wonderfully. I apologized for my sin of divisiveness, immorality and deceit. Marvin forgave me and was excited to see me come back to God and the church. God has been so merciful to me. I was restored to God on September 2, 2007.

My relationship with Marvin took a radical turn for the better, and he asked me to share my testimony at a Sunday service. A few weeks later, he entrusted me to preach with another brother as we spent hours going over the materials and ideas for the lesson. Then we went over to his house and practiced our whole sermon, focusing on mannerisms and tools for more effective presentation. God allowed this sermon to bless about 400 people. A few days later, Marvin had a vision that I could be a keynote speaker at a Single's Conference in four months time. I was shocked and honored to be considered as a keynote speaker at the conference where 3,000 would be in attendance. I felt confident because I had been empowered by extensive training and prayer.

Again, we spent hours in preparation, and the week before the conference, I preached my message to our congregation. Afterward, I asked for input from those who heard the message, and we spent a few more hours fine-tuning the speech before the conference. When the conference finally arrived, I felt God's hand and full support all around me. God moved powerfully, and hearts were moved at the conference by what I had to say. I learned later that Marvin had been in the ministry for sixteen years and had never spoken to a crowd of that size. He co-directed the conference and could have put himself forward as a keynote speaker, but chose instead to empower me to encourage the singles from all over the world with my message.

Never in my wildest dream had I thought I would be able to serve in such a way! I knew I could not have done this without God, and this proved to me that God believed in me, and that he communicated this through the faith and vision of the leaders of his people. Who would have thought that, of all those people, Marvin would be the one to believe in me and help me accomplish something that otherwise I could have never imagined. God must have a sense of humor! My relationship with Marvin went from an outright hateful one to one that has helped me grow in my ability to lead others and maximize the talents God has given me to bring him glory.

At the time of this writing, I am still working as a teacher, and my faith is at an all-time high. I now lead forty singles in the church and look for every opportunity to lead. It is painful to reflect on my sin and how it caused me to leave the church, but I understand now that I needed life's discipline to have the pure heart and sincere motives that I have today. I would like to conclude with these Scriptures:

> *Consider it pure joy, my brothers, whenever you face trials of many kinds, because you know that the testing of your faith develops perseverance. Perseverance must finish its work so that you may be mature and complete, not lacking anything* (James 1:2-4).

> *Blessed is the man who perseveres under trial, because when he has stood the test, he will receive the crown of life that God has promised to those who love him* (James 1:12).

Author's note: Carlos left as an older son and came back as the younger son, broken but celebrated.[107]

Conclusion: Empowering Prayer

> When we rely upon organization, we get what organization can do; when we rely upon education, we get what education can do; when we rely upon eloquence, we get what eloquence can do, and so on. Nor am I disposed to undervalue any of these things in their proper place, but when we rely upon prayer, we get what God can do.[108]

Our exegetical entrustment journey started in this book with Jesus spending all night on a mountainside praying to select his twelve leaders who would turn this world upside-down. It is only fitting then to end this book focusing in on the power of prayer that truly changes others. Personally, I do not consider myself a prayerful man, but I pray. It seems as I get older, I rely less on myself and more on God, which drives me to prayer. For anyone to reach their true potential in any relationship—in their marriage, in their parenting or in their leadership ability, they must draw from God's wisdom and transformation power. Paul understood that praying for others was the true power behind a miraculous life-changing process:

> *I pray that out of his glorious riches he may strengthen you with power through his Spirit in your inner being, so that Christ may dwell in your hearts through faith. And I pray that you, being rooted and established in love, may have the power* (Ephesians 3:16-18).

God has the power! Prayer changes one's "inner being." The most untrusting heart can be broken by hours of prayer and fasting. I have seen this in others and in my own life. My wife, who is a prayerful woman, prayed that my atheistic heart would break, and it did. I have had my life threatened by "Christians" to the point that my wife was fearful to leave the house. There have been many times when I have fallen on my knees to find the energy and heart to not give up on an individual.[109] The greatest weapon Satan uses to stop the empowering process is to get us to have a lack of longsuffering love and a sincere reliance on God.[110] Remember: resentment and bitterness are *anti*-trust.

If this book has stirred your spirit and you know that you do not have an empowering heart, please begin spending an hour on your knees every day because that can change you. Pray for clarity and a new heart to love others; without forgiveness, there is no trust—which is always the first step of entrustment. God changes people; I am living proof of this.

> "Beware in your prayers, above everything else, of limiting God, not only by unbelief, but by fancying that you know what He can do. Expect unexpected things, 'above all that we ask or think'. Each time, before you intercede, be quiet first, and worship God in His glory. Think of what He can do, and how He delights to hear the prayers of His redeemed people. Think of your place and privilege in Christ, and expect great things!"[111]

Appendix
I

Entrustment Evaluation

For by the grace given me I say to every one of you: Do not think of yourself more highly than you ought, but rather think of yourself with sober judgment, in accordance with the measure of faith God has given you (Romans 12:3).

I wrote down this list, not as a to-do list for you to use to develop a "quick-fix entrusting strategy," but so you can see where you are as an entruster/trainer. A person should already have or be living out many of these virtues, but remember, it is not a regiment—it should be your heart and life. Remember, above all, entrustment always starts with faith and trust! Please, evaluate yourself before you impose this on others.[112]

Personal Evaluation

Am I an "Entruster"?

- Whom do I really trust? Write down names.
- Am I completely open with these people about my sin and weaknesses?
- Do I give to others, not expecting anything back?
- Have I stopped loving people because they stopped giving to me?

Leadership Questions:

- Do you feel that raising up leaders is the future of our society/church?
- Write down a list of empowerers that you know (look for all the signs of an entruster).
- Who are you raising up?
- Write down the names. Do they know the personal vision you have for them?
- Are these individuals just like you (same upbringing, race and worldview)? Remember, we must become all things to all people.[113]
- Are you walking (or talking) with them daily?
- Are you personally supervising your protégé appointments and giving real-time instruction afterwards?
- What is your plan to develop their leadership ability? Do they know this plan?
- Does the church or ministry group know this plan?
- Are you making yourself *less* and them *more*?
- If you are raising someone up, do they share in teaching opportunities or in public leadership forums?
- Are you giving them everything you know and have without expecting something in return (besides their growth)?
- Remember, they must be trained in every aspect of the job you do (no exceptions).

Signs of an Entruster

- Your fruits are multiplied in others and visible to all.
- You should have several recent examples of your empowerment (write down names).
- Has a daily relationship and excellent communication with their apprentice.

- Shows no sentimentality or favoritism to the apprentice.
- Is not a one-man show.
- Gives constant hands-on training (getting in the trenches).
- Makes themselves less and others more.
- Is not in front as much, and will give their apprentice every opportunity to shine and to be trained.
- Sets their apprentice up for success in every situation, with ample training, to gain respect and trust from peers.
- Treats their apprentice not as an intern/youth minister but as the "future you" and much more.
- Teaching and training is a way of life, not a program or assignment.
- Communicates to others the plan and intention of the protégé's development.
- Has a history of seeing the abilities in the young, and raising people up.
- Is loyal and faithful through transitions and setbacks (vital).
- Communicates their detailed intentions and vision from the beginning (not haphazardly).
- Gives the protégé more and more responsibility over time, with sufficient training.
- Remembers their apprentice can do everything the master can do and even more, given time and training.
- Is open about their own sin and develops a safe place for the apprentice to challenge the entruster's conduct when it needs to be challenged.

Signs of an Entrustee
- Has at least six months as a Christian.
- Has raw leadership skills and ability.
- Possesses good communication skills and communicates in a timely and responsible manner.

- Has the time and willingness to be trained.
- Cares for others and serves without prompting.
- Has a spiritual mindset.
- Has a concern for the "lostness" of others (they share their faith without prompting).
- Is open about weaknesses and sin.
- Respects peers and those whom they serve.
- Has shown a character to overcome (while in the church).
- Trusts your leadership and will follow (assuming you are a worthy example).
- Is reliable (look for timeliness and follow-through on their word).
- Will follow direction (start with smaller assignments to see if they follow in detail).
- Must be humble when challenged.
- Has an opinion and is not a people-pleaser.
- Is inspired by a personal vision and embraces challenges (with God).

A Marriage of Entrustment

Have your spouse answer the same questions.

- Do I trust my spouse? (If you cannot say yes to this question, I would seek counseling as a couple, first. Remember that without trust, there is no entrustment).[114]
- Would your spouse feel that he/she is in an empowering marriage?
- Do you show compassion when an offense is committed and trust the heart and intention of your spouse?

Husband, are you...

- Leading your wife spiritually (ask her)?
- Open about shortcomings and showing humility in your marriage?

- Initiating spiritual dialog and resolution?
- In tune with the emotional and spiritual development of your wife?
- Intentional in having a spiritual plan for your spouse?

Wife, do you...

- Make your husband's role easy (Ephesians 5)?
- Have a heart of Jesus to be long-suffering and still believe in your husband?
- Remember that you are the wind beneath his wings?
- Tell your children how great their father is?
- Assignment: Write down all the positive attributes of your husband, and share them with him.

Parents, as a couple...

- Are you the biggest fans of your kids?
- Do you have an intentional spiritual plan for each of your kids?
- Does your spouse know of this plan?
- Would you still love your child if they have a totally different worldview than you?
- Would you still love your child if they chose a different faith or church than you?
- Would you still love your child if they dropped out of school or had poor grades?
- Do you and your spouse have monthly meetings to discuss the development of your child's spiritual character?
- Ask your child if he/she feels your unconditional love for them.
- Is your child open about their inner feelings with at least one of their parents?
- Does your family have weekly times to discuss family issues and set guidelines as situations come up?

- If you have a pre-teesn, do you have a set weekly relational time with each child?
- If you have teens, does your household have "pre-prodigal" rules established?

Appendix

II

Norwich, England
My Hometown Mission

Introduction

I grew up in the city of Norwich with a population of 300,000. Located 100 miles northeast of London, Norwich is known for its mustard and its tenth-century Norman castle. Norwich prides itself in its religious history and has a cathedral that has been standing for a thousand years. I spent twenty-two years of my life there, never going to church or having a Bible in my home. Now, twenty years later, having become a Christian and having seventeen years of ministerial experience and six years of formal theological schooling, I have a burning desire to give back to my hometown. Many who envision England still believe that this nation is a religious stronghold. Great Britain in the 18th century was a religious powerhouse, fueled by great preachers like William Carey, John and Charles Wesley, John Knox and David Livingstone. These men evangelized India, Asia and the Americas. But in the 21st century, this is far from the truth.

21st Century Christianity in England

Norwich is steeped in religious history and there are several stories of the city in *Foxes Christian Martyrs of the World*. One story involves Simon Miller, who in 1557 was a local trader who did business in Norwich. Because he was a man of faith and would speak openly against Catholicism, he was later arrested and brought before the Chancellor. During the hearing, Chancellor Dunning asked him to recant, but Miller stood firm and so was sentenced to be burned at the stake. On July 30, 1557, Miller was led out; and with him was a young lady named Elizabeth Cooper who was also condemned for the same crime. The location for this punishment was the St. Andrews Church, located in the center of Norwich. The Chancellor read the crime to the on-looking crowd and the fires were lit. Elizabeth was afraid and she began to cry out. Miller put his hand out towards her, telling her to be strong and of good cheer: "For, good sister," he said, "we shall have a joyful meeting hereafter." This reassured her and they both stood still and quietly committed their souls to the Lord.[115]

Why is this story so personal to me? It was at St. Andrew (Hall) where I would party in Norwich. In my adolescence, I remember collapsing in a drunken stupor during a party in this church building! Today, it is ironic how this place of radical religious fervor is now a place of sin and debauchery. This describes the religious landscape of England today. Another alarming statistic of the decline of faith in this country is in the church closures.

> Methodist Chapels: In the last 75 years, somewhere in the region of 8,000 Methodist chapels have been closed. Many of these were constructed in the 19th century and being smaller than Church of England churches are more suitable to conversion as a single home.[116]

Churches being converted into homes are the new eclectic way of living, especially in London: *The Royal Institution of Chartered Surveyors (RICS) says that in the last 5 years, around 500 London churches have been turned into homes.*[117] Churches have been converted into bars and restaurants.[118] One conversion that caused a stir was in the small town of Clitheroe in England where the city council approved a Methodist Church to be converted to a Mosque![119] In places like Blackburn, the constituency of Jack Straw, the leader of the *House of Commons*, there are 30,000 Muslims among a population of 80,000. But in a telltale sign of the future, the number of children

10 years and younger is evenly divided between Christian and Muslim families.[120] I read on BBC's religious website that "Church attendances have been dropping and only 4% of the population goes to church."[121] Between the ages of 15–30, attendees are virtually non-existent. Britain may continue to regard itself as a "Christian nation," but practicing Muslims are likely to outnumber church-attending Christians in several decades, according to a recent survey by *Christian Research,* a group that specializes in documenting the status of Christianity in Britain.[122] In some cities, you can even see the skyline peppered with as many mosques as there are churches.

As another sign of what may be to come, many of the youth today are reverting back to paganism. In my last visit to Edinburgh, there were hundreds of students involved in Beltane, which includes festivals and rituals that "awaken elements of Air, Earth, Water and Fire." This movement caters to the mystic and environmental awareness of this postmodern generation. It is sad to see such a spiritual void in England that is regressing back to hedonistic practices. The future of Christianity looks bleak in Britain, but sometimes in the deepest darkness, light shines the brightest.

From my research and several years of preaching and teaching in England, I have developed a missional strategy. Wagner stresses that the mission must have a "cutting edge" approach,[123] meaning that one must keep in step with the Spirit and learn as we go.[124] There is nothing like experience and learning from the knocks and bruises of everyday ministry. I find that today's church programs are filled with questionnaires and rote answers, which produce a sterile environment and shallow relations. What is missing from our society today is sincerity. The following passages elaborate on this point:

> *Love must be sincere. Hate what is evil; cling to what is good. Be devoted to one another in brotherly love. Honor one another above yourselves* (Romans 12:9-10).

> *Above all, love each other deeply, because love covers over a multitude of sin*s (1 Peter 4:8).

A true and sincere love for the lost is missing in most programs. When we have to go to a class to love the lost, we have lost! Our outreach should be an overflow of one's salvation and God's grace:

> *So then, just as you received Christ Jesus as Lord, continue to live in him, rooted and built up in him, strengthened in the faith as you were taught, and overflowing with thankfulness* (Colossians 2:6-7).

I spent the Christmas of 2007 in Norwich. My wife and I visited two churches while we were there, one of which was a Methodist Church several hundred years old. It was very orthodox and I quite enjoyed it, because when I was a child, our school choir sang a hymn in that church. The average age of the parishioners was sixty years old, and only fifty people were in attendance. This service drove my wife crazy, with their emblems and sacraments. So we left and went to another church about 100 yards from where I used to live as a child. We entered the church and to our surprise, we saw young faces and a band playing. The minister started to preach and he had an American accent. I was shocked! This church was a planting two years ago from America. I enjoyed the preaching, and when he had finished, he asked everyone to come down to the front and kneel. All the members left their seats and knelt before the preacher (we stayed in our seats).

The preacher started to speak in "tongues" (it was not a comprehensible language). After the service concluded, people were very warm and reached out to us. One observation that I made was that the minister's message had a lot of illustrations from an American perspective. The minister had not assimilated to the British culture and came across more as a foreigner. The minister also showed a lack of connectivity to the locals. These two snapshots show where England is today—either Orthodox or over the top! My parents, who are nonbelievers, would not have liked either one of these services.

This charismatic church models itself after the American Pentecostal movement. Here in America, we see a decline of Christianity[125] and also in Britain.[126] My question is why anyone would imitate something that has proven to be flawed? True discipleship starts with a calling and then a time of walking with someone, sometimes for several years. This type of discipleship takes a mentor who is worthy of imitation and has excellent relational skills. George Patterson's views on discipleship are stated thusly: "Teach and practice obedience to Jesus' commands in love, above all else." He continues by saying that a church must start out with intimate discipleship from the beginning.[127] Most churches try to engraft discipleship but meet with little success. In order for it to work, it must be intentional from the inception of the church. Today, many look for programs and the latest Evangelical trends. Nothing will or should ever surpass the ministry that Jesus established of walking with others.[128] The English are starving for relational discipleship.

Hope for the Future

As a minister, I have spoken several times in Britain, including over the same holiday period described earlier, during which I spoke at two churches in London. It was refreshing to see the spirit of the people. My own church group has slowed down in growth due to a corporate and impersonal paradigm emanating from the United States back in the late 90s. Due to this rough past, our English churches now have a low view of leadership, yet they are lacking the training and direction that once came from America. They find themselves in a quandary. Considering my past and training, I am becoming more involved with these churches, because I understand the people of England and the cultural challenges.

While speaking in London and other churches in Great Britain, I have crossed paths with those who once lived in Norwich or were actually born there. These individuals have shown great interest to go to Norwich on a mission trip. My original timeline for this mission planting was for it to take place when my kids were in college, when my wife and I would be free to go over for several months to build a church. The mission team's initial outreach would be to our natural mission field, the family and friends with whom we grew up. To win them to Christ, we will use our own spiritual formation and our experience with the Norwich people. There will be no programs but true discipleship. The gospel will be shared by our mouths and lives. People will be trained by walking with one another. Paul shared this ministry pattern with the church in Thessalonica: "We loved you so much that we were delighted to share with you not only the gospel of God but our lives as well, because you had become so dear to us" (1 Thessalonians 2:8).

Opening our homes and our lives shows true trust in others. This relational foundation will build a sincere fellowship. The ministry will be based on empowering one another to rely on the Holy Spirit and God's love. Jesus spoke about the power of the Holy Spirit in these words: "But the Counselor, the Holy Spirit, whom the Father will send in my name, will teach you all things and will remind you of everything I have said to you" (John 14:26). With the help of the Holy Spirit, we will have energetic services with a traditional twist which will bridge the generational gap. Sound biblical preaching that relates to the local people and their context will also help them to connect to Jesus. This is my plan, but there is always the Lord's plan!

Author's Note: Indeed the Spirit has moved and our family will be moving to England shortly and planting the church in Norwich in the summer of 2011.

Conclusion

If one did a Web search on Norwich and Religion, they would find the name "Julian of Norwich." In May 1373, she allegedly received sixteen revelations from God. From these revelations, she wrote a book called "*he Revelation of Divine Love.*"[129] This book is about God's love and the lost having a relationship with him. In her book, she laments, "I speak of them that shall be saved, for in this time God shewed me none other. But in all things I believe as Holy Church believeth, preacheth, and teacheth."[130] My heart is like Julian's to go back to Norwich to preach and teach God's Word so that my people "shall be saveth."[131]

All my proceeds from this book are going to Norwich Missions. In the recent months, God has open doors for me to fulfill a life-long dream in planting a church in my hometown of Norwich in 2011. If you want to help in the missional work personally or give financial support or just get updates, go to **www.norwichchurch.org.**

Please, keep us and the church in your prayers.

Endnotes

1 Oswald Chambers.
2 Author Unknown.
3 Adapted from a sermon by Dave Hartson.
4 Matthew 5:2.
5 Matthew 13:22.
6 Luke 8:14.
7 Revelation 3:17.
8 Matthew 6:19-21.
9 Colossians 2 and Ephesians 5.
10 Acts 2:41.
11 Luke 14:32-33.
12 Romans 3:2.
13 1 Corinthians 4:1.
14 Romans 2:16.
15 1 Corinthians 4:2.
16 Matthew 16.
17 Mark 9:19.
18 1 Peter 2:23.
19 John 14:12.
20 Mark 16:14.
21 Hebrews 12:4-11.
22 Matthew 17:17.
23 W. Phillip Keller.
24 Revelation 3:16.
25 Hebrews 12:15.
26 Acts 1:8.
27 Acts 2:38.
28 John 16:7, 13.

[29] John 14:15, 21.

[30] Acts 1:8.

[31] George F. Jowett, *The Drama of the Lost Disciples*, (London: Covenant Publishing Co., Ltd., 1970), 176..

[32] William Byron Forbush. Editor, *Fox's Book of Martyrs*, (New York: Holt, Rinehart and Winston, 1926).

[33] *Fox's Book of Martyrs*, Ibid.

[34] *Fox's Book of Martyrs*, Ibid.

[35] Acts 15:39.

[36] 2 Timothy 2:2.

[37] 2 Timothy 3:11; 4:9.

[38] 2 Timothy 4:10.

[39] Acts 17.

[40] 1 Thessalonians 3:5-6.

[41] James 4:13-16.

[42] Acts 7.

[43] Luke 9:51-56.

[44] Acts 6.

[45] Galatians 1:18.

[46] John 14:12.

[47] Dietrich Bonhoeffer.

[48] George Barna, *The Power of Team Leadership*, (Colorado Springs, CO: Waterbrook Press, 2001), 34-35.

[49] Quotes from Rob's Bell: *Velvet Elvis*, (Grand Rapdis, MI: Zondervan Publishing, 2005), 110-116.

[50] Charisma, 10/23/03

[51] John 12:24.

[52] Greg Ogden, *Transforming Discipleship*, (Downers Grove, IL:, InterVarsity Press, 2003), 43.

[53] 1 Peter 1:22.

[54] James 5:16.

[55] Hebrews 3:12.

[56] 2 Samuel 12:1-7.

57 Philippians 2:12-13.
58 David Marrow, *Why Men Hate Going to Church*, (Nashville, Tenn:, Thomas Nelson, Inc., 2005).
59 Colossians 1:10-12.
60 George Barna, *Revolution*, (Tyndale House Publishers, 2005), 8.
61 Kenton C. Anderson.
62 C. Campbell Morgan (1863-1945).
63 Mark 1:17; Luke 8:1.
64 1 Corinthians 9:22-23.
65 1 Peter 2:21.
66 2 Corinthians 12:18, *New Living Translation*.
67 Paul J. Meyers.
68 Ephesians 6:4.
69 Matthew 28:18-20.
70 Luke 15:32.
71 Ephesians 6:4.
72 1 Corinthians 15:33.
73 James 1:14-15.
74 Galatians 5:9.
75 2 Corinthians 4:16-18.
76 Romans 12:9.
77 Proverbs 25:21.
78 Romans 12:12.
79 Matthew 6:15.
80 Luke 15:20.
81 Romans 12:12.
82 The Minneola Messenger.
83 Ruth Harms Calkin.
84 Ephesians 5:23.
85 1 Peter 3:6.
86 Proverbs 17:19.
87 Ephesians 5:27.
88 Luke 24:11.

[89] John 20:26.

[90] Mark 14:16.

[91] Ephesians 5:33.

[92] The Bible Friend.

[93] 1 Corinthians 15:33.

[94] Proverbs 31.

[95] Matthew 5:44-88.

[96] 1 Peter 1:22.

[97] Hebrews 12:3; Ephesians 4:25-27.

[98] 1 Corinthians 13:1 (*The Message*): States that we are just making obnoxious noise when there is no love in our hearts.

[99] John McDowell.

[100] Sermoncentral.com.

[101] 1 John 4:18.

[102] Our Daily Bread.

[103] Luke 8:45.

[104] Luke 8:48.

[105] 1 Timothy 5:2; Ephesians 5:3.

[106] Matthew 18:15.

[107] Luke 15.

[108] A. C. Dixon.

[109] Matthew 5:44.

[110] 1 Corinthians 13:17.

[111] Andrew Murray.

[112] Matthew 7:5.

[113] 1 Corinthians 9:22.

[114] 1 Corinthians 13:6-7.

[115] William Byron Forbush. Editor, *Fox's Book of Martyrs*, (New York: Holt, Rinehart and Winston, 1926).

[116] *Church Closures Statistics*, www.eauk.org.

[117] *Church Conversions to Homes*, www.ourproperty.co.uk.

[118] *Thousands of Churches Face Foreclosure*, www.timesonline.co.uk.

[119] *Churches converted to Mosque*, Sweetness-light.com.uk.

[120]Sweetness-light.com.uk.

[121] *BBC Religion and Ethics Stats*, www.bbc.co.uk/religion/religions.

[122] Ibid.

[123] C. Peter Wagner, *Perceptions*, 533.

[124] Galatians 5:25.

[125] George Barna, *Revolution*, (Tyndale House Publishers, 2005), 8.

[126] BBC Religion and Ethics.

[127] George Patterson, *Perspective*, 601.

[128] Mark 1:17.

[129] Livingstone, 323.

[130] *The Revelations of Divine Love*, 11.

[131] Ibid., 11.

RESOURCES FROM GORDON FERGUSON

The Power of Gratitude

Gratitude is not just something nice to have. Gratitude is a pure and powerful expression of humility that transforms the mind and enriches the lives of those who see and feel it. Life has its negative elements, and many choose to focus on these with a complaining spirit. In a world where cynical and caustic comments seem to fill the air, some old-fashioned gratitude is badly needed.

In this insightful volume, Gordon Ferguson, a much-loved teacher and elder, shares lessons and examples from his own life. Some are heart warming, some are challenging. All of them help us to see ways in which we need to be grateful and show us the divine power that gratitude brings to our lives. This book brings into focus the life-changing power of gratitude that can change us to the core of our beings.

Price: $10.00 • 164 page softcover book • ISBN: 1577821246

Mine Eyes Have Seen the Glory
The Victory of the Lamb
in the Book of Revelation

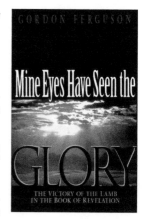

Mysterious. Confusing. Intriguing. Symbolic. Deep. Difficult. Literal. Futuristic. All these words and many others describe the final book of the Bible.

Misunderstood. Misinterpreted. Misapplied. These words speak of the "missed" message of Revelation in light of today's prevailing humanism, hedonism and hypocrisy.

Inspiring. Crucial. Radical. Victorious. Compelling. Challenging. Thrilling. Strengthening. These are a few of the right words—God's initial intent—about what is to happen in our hearts and in our souls after spending time with the apostle John on the island of Patmos as he reveals God through this revelation. In *Mine Eyes Have Seen the Glory*, Gordon Ferguson unlocks and unleashes God's powerful and timeless message—a message that will forever revolutionize our lives!

Price: $14.00 • 196 page softcover book • ISBN: 188453923

Available at www.ipibooks.com

RESOURCES FROM GORDON FERGUSON

Soul-ed Out
A Video Workshop for Devoted Living

A recent study compared the lifestyles of those who claimed to be Christians and those who had no religious affiliation. Whether it was in the area of marriage and divorce, abortion, sexual immorality or integrity, there was no appreciable difference in those who claimed to be Christians and those who did not. It's obvious the religious world has lost touch with the genuine call of faith. In this powerful video series, Gordon calls listeners back to the meaning of making Jesus the Lord of their lives.

Four Video Lessons (approximately 1 hour each).

1. Called Out: *Exploring the significance and implications of being uniquely chosen by God.*

2. Poured Out: *How to make relationships that will help us change and change the world.*

3. Sold Out: *Why God desires total commitment to his Lordship and how to make that a reality in our lives.*

4. Go Out: *How to restore our love for the lost and help people become true disciples of Christ.*

Price: $12.00 • Four Hours (2 DVDS) • ISBN: 9780981737386

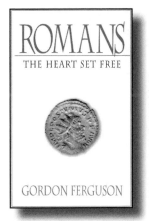

Romans
The Heart Set Free

Religion binds us. Grace and faith set us free. In large part, this is the message of the letter to the Romans. Considered by many to be Paul's greatest written work, Romans shows us the power of sin, the failure of normal religion to deal with it and the absolute victory we can have over it through faith in the blood that was shed on the cross.

In this book, Gordon Ferguson delves into what he believes just may be the most important book in Scripture. Gordon willl help you to understand the message of this great epistle as never before—and this understanding can set your heart free. What is more, once you get Romans, God gets you!

Price: $12.00 • 200 page softcover book • ISBN: 1577821688

Available at www.ipibooks.com

Illumination Publishers International

Toney Mulhollan has worked in Christian publishing for 35 years. He has served as the Production Manager for Crossroads Publications, Discipleship Magazine/Upside Down Magazine, Discipleship Publications International (DPI) and on the production teams of Campus Journal, Biblical Discipleship Quarterly, Bible Illustrator and others.

Toney serves as Executive Editor of Illumination Publishers International. He is happily married to the love of his life, Denise L. Mulhollan, M.D. They make their home in Houston, Texas along with their daughters, Audra Joan and Cali Owen.

For the best in Christian writing and audio instruction, go to the Illumination Publishers website. We're commited to producing in-depth teaching that will inform, inspire and encourage Christians to a deeper and more committed walk with God. You can reach Toney Mulhollan by email at toneyipibooks@mac.com.

www.ipibooks.com

ipi